How to Make Pottery

How to Make Pottery

BY HERBERT H. SANDERS, Ph.D
PROFESSOR IN CERAMIC ART,
SAN JOSE STATE UNIVERSITY

WATSON-GUPTILL PUBLICATIONS, NEW YORK

Library of Congress Cataloging in Publication Data
Sanders, Herbert H.
    How to make pottery.
    First ed. published in 1953 under title: Sunset
ceramics book; 2d ed. published in 1964 under title:
How to make pottery and ceramic sculpture.
    Bibliography: p.
    1. Pottery craft. I. Title.
TT920.S26 1974   738.1   73–20020
ISBN 0–8230–2420–2

3 4 5 6 7 8 9/86 85 84 83 82

Originally published 1964 under the title *How to Make Pottery and Ceramic Sculpture*
by Lane Books, Menlo Park, California (© 1964 by Lane Magazine and Book Company),
with some material previously published in *Sunset Ceramics Book* (© 1953).

ACKNOWLEDGMENTS

The author wishes to acknowledge his gratitude to the many students and friends who contributed to this book. Many students at The California State University at San Jose as well as professors of ceramics contributed examples of processes and completed ware. I have tried to include the name of the artist along with the photographed example.

Where glaze compositions are presented they were provided by the individual whose name accompanies the composition. Other glaze compositions were provided by the author.

Process-sequence photos were provided by Gene Kenefick, Joseph L. Hysong, Maryann Gravitt, Philip Cornelius, Joseph Hawley, Jan Jones, Doris Aller, Professor Claude Horan, John Leary, James Lovera, and Robert Fritz. The following photographers took most of the sequence pictures: Robert Fritz, Gene Kenefick, Claude Horan, Joseph M. Campbell, Charles Mulkey, Fred W. K. Hamilton, Wes Hammond, and Marvin Wax. Ernie Kim's lamp was photographed by Associated Press, Mrs. Aller's work by her husband, Paul Aller, and Mrs. Palmer's by her husband Phil Palmer.

The following photographers provided new pictures for this edition: John Bobeda (pages 12, 20, 22, 38, 45, 49, 52, 68, 73, 79, 84, 85, 86, 90, 91, 102, 116), Fred Gaeden (pages 75, 76), Otto Hagel (page 83), and Fran Ortiz (page 79, 81). The diagrams on pages 100–101 are by Robert E. Johnson.

Contents

Introduction

Clay is a basic craft medium, and making pottery is one of our most popular crafts. It is undoubtedly the gentle nature of this medium that accounts for much of the popularity of the craft—soft, moist clay, plastic and pliable, is so easily formed into sturdy pottery pieces. The satisfying results achieved through the most elementary effort make clay an ideal medium for those who seek a craft activity for relaxation during leisure hours, as well as for those who will use it for educational or therapeutic purposes.

This book describes the methods and materials used to make pottery by hand processes. It is intended as a manual of self-instruction for the beginner who will work at home, as supplementary material for both student and teacher in the classroom, and for use in therapy and rehabilitation done in community centers and hospitals.

Although parts of this book will interest potters at any stage of achievement and experience, it is also written with the complete novice in mind. The preliminary steps in learning the pottery-making processes are presented in a sequence that corresponds to developing abilities. Later steps, although not often undertaken by the beginner working alone, will provide an understanding of all phases of the craft and permit him to make a better beginning in it.

Stoneware coffee urn. Stained stoneware body, unglazed outside.

1
Ceramics as a Hobby

The craft of pottery making is being enthusiastically accepted by those who seek a pleasurable recreational activity, by those who want to add to their knowledge and skills in handicrafts, and by those who use crafts as a tool in teaching or therapy. Working with clay appeals to all these people, because the pliant, responsive material allows for achievement in some phase of the craft regardless of the degree of skill or ability of the worker.

Modern schools provide even the youngest pupils with soft clay for their creative play. As play material, clay has plastic properties that can be exploited without thought of an end product—the pleasure in pinching and pushing the clay into various forms is sufficient. As a craft material, clay is shaped and put through the various processes needed to make it a finished, usable piece.

You discovered that shaping a plastic mixture of earth and water was fun when you made your first mudpie. You took your materials as and where you found them, and your product was "baked" by an obliging sun. In a sense, your mudpie experience was your initial introduction to ceramics.

The term "ceramic" properly applies to a vast number of products made by shaping moist clay or similar substances, which are then dried and subjected to temperatures high enough to give the finished article strength and permanence. Ceramic products therefore include bricks, sewer tile, and porcelain fittings, to name but a few. From this you can see that the craft of making pottery bowls, plates, and such pieces by hand occupies but a small corner in the broad field of ceramics. There is room in this field, however, for unlimited experimentation and achievement for the craftsman, whether beginner or experienced potter.

This book is meant first of all for the novice who would like to try his hand at pottery making without acquiring expensive tools or equipment. It is quite possible to test the depth of your interest with a few pounds of moist pottery clay, a very few tools, and little equipment. You can be assured, too, that your very first efforts toward making things by hand with clay can be successful and satisfying. As in the practice of any craft, learning will come with doing. With each piece you make you will learn more about handling clay, and with each method you use you'll better appreciate the value of ceramics as a gratifying hobby.

The first important factor in the practice of any hobby is its basic raw material. In pottery this is clay. Clay is plentiful and inexpensive. You can buy it as dry powder and mix it with water, or you can buy it moist and ready for use. Clay is clean and easy to handle. It doesn't deteriorate and is easy to care for and store. If it becomes too dry to work, water will make it soft and pliable again, and spills and splashes can be wiped up with a water-dampened sponge. Clay can be reconditioned and reworked indefinitely until it has been fired.

The hands and fingers are the main "tools" used by the potter, regardless of the shaping method he uses. Direct handling of the material is especially desirable for the beginner as a method of "getting acquainted." The few essential tools and minimum equipment needs for use in any of the handbuilding methods are listed in the following chapter.

Large covered stoneware jar displays boldly incised decoration. Jerry Meek

Each pottery piece, however formed, must undergo certain kinds of treatment and phases of handling before it becomes a finished product. A little advance knowledge of these somewhat interlocked processes will be of benefit whether or not you choose to undertake them all as you make your first pieces.

In reading the following brief descriptions of ceramic processes, note the words which are a part of the special vocabulary of pottery work. At some time in the craft's long history these words and phrases may have been a part of the everyday language. Now they have specific meanings rather than general ones.

Pots. As a starting example, the potter refers to all clay pieces in the making, with the exception of sculptures, as pots and to his operations in making these as potting.

Throwing. Pots formed on the potter's wheel are spoken of as thrown and the work of making them as throwing.

Wedging. Before a mass of clay is used to make any piece, either handbuilt or wheel-thrown, it is first cut, smacked, and slapped in a vigorous manner to expel any air bubbles and to bring it to an even consistency throughout. This treatment, called wedging, serves the further purpose of removing any extraneous matter that may have been accidentally incorporated in the clay during previous handling. Wedging is an essential step and is fully explained and illustrated in a later chapter.

Shaping. When properly wedged, clay is ready for shaping. The obliging nature of the material allows it to take practically any shape. As you become sensitive to your material, however, you will find that shapes with soft curves and rounded corners and edges are the most pleasing and practical.

If work is interrupted at this stage, or a project is too large to complete at one sitting, wrap a damp cloth around the clay and cover it with an upturned bucket or box to keep it from drying out. When resuming work, moisten any stiffened edges before adding fresh clay.

Drying. When shaping of the piece is completed, set it aside to dry. Evaporation of the water in the clay will cause it to shrink as it dries. If shrinkage is sudden or occurs more rapidly in one part of the pot than another, it may warp or crack. Drying should therefore be slow and the piece shielded from drafts and sunlight. A cardboard carton inverted over the piece will make a temporary drying box if closed cupboard space isn't available.

When the clay pieces have become "leather-hard" (when the pieces can be handled without misshaping but are not dry), spouts, handles, and foot rims can be added. Some forms of decoration, such as "slip" glazes, carving, and modeled decoration, are also done when the piece is leather-hard. After the moisture content of the added parts and the form itself have equalized in a protected area or closed container, the piece may be set out to dry at room temperature.

Greenware. Plastic, leather-hard, or dry pottery pieces are known as greenware. A piece in any of these states is delicate and should be lifted and moved with care. Any attempt to grasp or lift it by the rim, handle, or spout will likely be disastrous to the piece, although the clay can be reworked. Instead, lift greenware from under or around its base, using both hands.

Kiln Firing. When greenware is thoroughly air-dried, it is ready for firing in a pottery kiln. Kiln firing could be likened to baking in an oven, except that firing temperatures for pottery clays greatly exceed those possible in a domestic stove. Although it is extremely desirable for the potter to own and operate his own kiln, the beginner can bypass this part of the work by having greenware fired at a ceramic studio which offers this service. Your ceramic supply dealer can give you information on having work custom-fired in your community.

Bisque Firing. Some pottery needs to be fired only once to make it fit its purpose. The first firing, known as the bisque, or biscuit, firing is the only one needed for the familiar terra-cotta flower pot, for example. Biscuit ware is usually porous, with the natural color of the clay used, and somewhat rough. Nevertheless, bisque-fired clay colors and textures are often pleasing for flower pots, fountains, sculptures, and other pieces with functions unimpeded by porosity, and these need no further treatment to make them complete.

The warm, toast-like colors created when stoneware is reduced make unglazed surfaces very popular. Functional forms of stoneware can be biscuited at low temperatures, glazed inside, and reduction fired at the appropriate stoneware firing temperature.

Glazing. Other pottery pieces are pleasing in use and appearance only if they have been coated with a glaze. The glaze coating serves to seal surfaces and make them smooth, as well as to add

Lamp base of slab construction with incised decoration. Ernie Kim

13

By using molds, the pottery-maker can duplicate useful items such as this ash tray which was cast in a two-piece mold.

Coil-built pieces may be utilitarian or decorative, symmetrical or non-symmetrical. Color of owl is terra cotta and white. Louise Pfeiffer

color. In most cases glaze coatings are applied to biscuit ware and the piece is then returned to the kiln for the "glost" fire which completes the piece.

Glazes are coatings of glass produced by the fusion of various compounded materials. In the raw state they appear as powders; when mixed with water for use, they become thin creamy pastes in pale tints. The glaze mixture is applied to biscuit ware with a soft brush by dipping or spraying the piece, or by pouring the glaze over it. Color and surface textures of the glaze develop in the glost firing.

Glazes, in unlimited colors and kinds, are for sale by your ceramic supply dealer. The beginner who is working alone will usually choose from these prepared and ready-to-use glazes and will have glazed pieces custom-fired.

From the preceding descriptions, given very briefly here but expanded in detail in later chapters, you can see that pottery making has many facets—any one of which may engage your eventual interest beyond all others. Some potters remain forever intrigued by the possibilities of shaping clay. Others find that their interest lies in firing it or in compounding glazes.

As a novice, you may doubt your ability to cover so many stages. Your doubts should disappear, however, when you realize how many people share your interest in ceramic crafts. Clay is being thumped and wedged, shaped and fired, in homes, studios, schools, hospitals, and community centers all over this land! If you need it, you'll find ready help in any phase of the work.

Basic tools include: modeling tools, rulers, sponges, oil cloth, piano wire, dividers, compass, rolling pin, bench whirler.

2
Tools and Materials

You will need a few inexpensive tools and several essential pieces of equipment before undertaking pottery making. You will also need a supply of clay. The clay, tools, and some of the equipment can be purchased from any dealer in ceramic supplies. Locate such dealers in your community through the classified section of the telephone book. Quantities of ceramic supplies can also be ordered by mail; you will find addresses of several mail order dealers in the Suppliers List in the back of this book. You may already have some of the essentials:

Work Table. The first essential is a substantial work table about 3' × 4' and about 30" high. The work surface can be unpainted wood, linoleum, or tempered composition board. It is often convenient to have a separate piece of composition board cut to tabletop size, thus adapting kitchen table to craft bench at will.

Clay Container. The clay container can be a 10-gallon stoneware crock with a lid or any small tub with cover. It is necessary to have the clay container covered to keep clay plastic and in good working condition. For mixing clay, glazes, and plaster you will need one or more enamel or stainless steel bowls or basins. An 8" mixing bowl is suitable.

Piano Wire. A piece of 20-gauge piano wire about 3' long—available from your ceramics supplies dealer or at large hardware stores—is needed for cutting clay in wedging.

Fettling Knife. A fettling knife is also useful. This has a long, narrow blade especially designed for

work with clay. Another clay-working tool is the wooden modeling tool. Buy one about 6" long which has one end flattened and rounded, the other end forming a flat angle.

Plastic Ruler. For making measurements, laying out circles, etc., provide yourself with a 12" plastic rule—wetting makes wooden ones useless—and a pair of dividers or a compass.

Rolling Pin. A wooden rolling pin and two pieces of wood ¼" × 1" × 18" are needed for rolling out slabs of clay; the narrow sticks are used as thickness guides.

Plaster Bat. Handbuilt pieces are generally easiest to turn and handle if they are begun on a porous unglazed base such as an unglazed tile or a plaster bat. Buy several unglazed tiles about 6" square from the ceramic supply dealer, or make a few plaster bats according to directions given in Chapter 3. Plaster bats are very helpful in working with clay. Clay that is too wet to work can be dried quickly by spreading it out on the bat, or wet bats can be placed under clay pieces to keep them damp between working periods.

Bench Whirler. Although not strictly necessary, a bench whirler, or banding wheel, sometimes called a modeling wheel, is very convenient to have. Work placed on a bat on the whirler makes it possible to view all sides of the piece easily, without need for the worker to move around it.

Ice Pick. An ice pick or sharp-pointed awl is needed for piercing holes or trimming rims of thrown pieces.

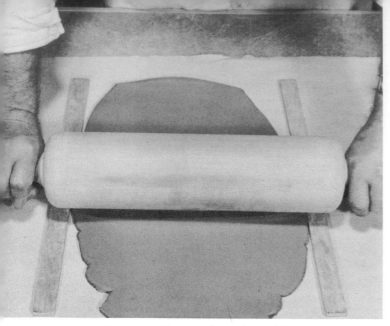

Common rolling pin for making slabs.

Plastic ruler not affected by moisture.

Elephant-ear sponge for finishing.

Sponge. For clean-up work and smoothing clay surfaces, you'll find that nothing works as well as the natural sponge. Have a small "elephant-ear" sponge for smoothing, moistening, and rounding edges, and a large synthetic sponge for lubricating clay and general clean-up.

Cheesecloth. Cheesecloth, surgical gauze, or worn sheeting can be used to wrap clay and unfinished pieces between work periods.

CHOOSING CLAY

The kind of clay you buy will depend on what you want to make with it and the firing conditions available. The latter is a most important consideration in selecting your clay. Do not, for instance, choose a clay which needs a high temperature to bring it to maturity if firing facilities available are limited to those in a lower range. If your first pieces are to be custom-fired, it will be wise to discuss the choice of clay with the kiln operator before making any purchase.

Varieties recommended according to use are pottery and modeling clay and sculpture clay. These are available in white, buff, and reddish terra cotta color familiar in common bricks and flowerpots. The clay particularly desired for larger sculptures contains an added percentage of "grog." Grog is ground-up particles of clay that has been fired. It can be purchased and added to a portion of the pottery clay to adapt it to sculptural uses.

Clay can be purchased in large or small amounts, either in a dry, powdered state or in a moist mass. The price per pound is less when it is purchased in larger quantities. As a starter, buy a 25- or 50-pound package of moist clay body put up in a plastic storage bag. The plastic bag will keep the clay in workable condition for months.

WHAT IS CLAY?

Some craftsmen may be curious about the properties and structure of clay; others may not be until they have handled and worked with it for a time. The following discussion will answer the question in simple terms for those who want to know more about clay than is actually needed merely to make a pot.

When the earth was formed, the dry land was but a rocky crust. Forces such as rain, winds, heat, and cold worked on the crust to break it down into soil. The rocks were of different kinds, and consequently soil formed from them was of different kinds. For instance, sand is soil formed from a kind of rock which breaks into millions of smaller rocks. A grain of sand is three-dimensional and may have sharp corners and many facets. A handful of fine, wet sand, squeezed together, will form a mass until the sand dries and the water evaporates. A chemist would say that the ions (atoms carrying electric charges) in the water hold the grains together; as soon as electric charges are lost, the sand mass falls apart.

Clay is a different kind of soil. The rock which forms clay is broken down into millions of extremely fine particles which are very thin and flat —like tiny sheets of paper or flat metal plates. Water causes these to stick together. A chemist would say that water increases molecular attraction between clay particles. A simple experiment illustrates this. Wet two flat sheets of glass and lay one atop the other. Lifting the top sheet without also lifting the bottom will be difficult. Try sliding one over the other, and you will find it comparatively easy. Flat, wet clay particles will slide but are held together by the molecular attraction of the water cushion. The result is a soft, pliable mass. This property in clay is known as "plasticity," and it is this that makes clay different from any other soil.

When powdered clay is mixed with water, not all of the tiny particles stack uniformly or fit together perfectly. Minute open spaces are left when particles stand on edge or sideways. These open spaces fill with water to form pores. This condition in clay is called porosity. The smaller the particles, the more of them there are to fit closely and slide; the pores will then be small and the clay very plastic. It may be necessary to add sand or other coarse material to make clay more porous— so that water can evaporate uniformly as it escapes —before this plastic clay can be successfully used by the potter. However, care should be taken not to add too much sand or the clay will be weakened. For instance, when a bowl dries the clay particles which form the walls pull togther as the water of the cushion between them evaporates. The walls of the bowl shrink as the clay crystals pull together. The clay becomes harder and stronger as it loses its plasticity, and the strength of the dry clay bowl is the result of the attraction of the flat clay crystal surfaces. If clay is too coarse-grained or contains an excessive amount of sand or other coarse material, the bowl will lack strength.

Should you put water in a dry clay bowl, it would disintegrate to become once again a soft

Wooden spatula for welding joints.

Calipers are used for measuring.

Piano wire separates ware from wheel.

Stoneware is fine-textured but sturdy; it becomes semi-vitrified at high temperatures.

mass of plastic clay. Before the form can become permanent it must be fired in a pottery kiln. Changes in the structure of the clay take place when it is fired. The particles pull together still more tightly than they did while simply drying. This is because drying dispelled the "water of plasticity." There is a second type of water in clay not evaporated by mere air drying. This is the chemically combined water which is a part of the clay particle, and it is the driving off of this water by heat that causes the clay to shrink still further in firing.

Clay in its pure state requires very high temperatures to become sufficiently rock-like to be durable—such high temperatures, in fact, that it is impractical to use pure clay alone to make ware.

Most clays contain many impurities. If clay is moved from the location in which it was formed, it picks up many more impurities in its travels; these become ground in with the clay particles. These impurities are usually of such a nature that they melt into glass when clay is fired, and the glass film binds pure clay together. Melting these impurities to make glass is the process known to the potter as "vitrification." The amount of vitrification depends on the amounts of glass-forming materials present and the temperature to which the wares are fired.

Some clays are formed by rocks which have been covered over by marshes and swamps. In the process, the decaying weeds and grasses formed carbonic acid and marsh gases. Acid, gases, and swamp water broke down the rock and dissolved the soluble materials in it, leaving a bed of comparatively pure clay. This clay is known as "primary" or "residual." Residual clays are usually refractory, which means that they withstand a very high degree of heat without melting. These clays usually fire white or pale cream color, are not very plastic, and must be blended with other clays and minerals for making ware. These are the clays used to make porcelain.

As other clays are formed by the breaking up of rocks, they are picked up and carried by streams and rivers—sometimes for great distances. As they travel, particles are ground finer and finer and join with fragments of other rocks such as limestone and vegetable matter. When the stream carrying the combined particles reaches a lake or settling area, a bed of "secondary," or "sedimentary," clay forms. Some sedimentary clay may be spoken of as "earthenware" clay. The group of earthenware clays includes most of the shales and surface clays prevalent in the eastern part of the United

States. These clays fire red or brown because of their high iron content. These red-burning clays are very fusible—when heated to the vitrification point they fuse and melt, and the ware loses shape because of the large percentage of impurities.

Sedimentary clays vary in that some do not travel so far or join up with the same particles on the way. One of these, containing a medium percentage of glass-forming impurities, is known as "stoneware" clay. Stoneware clays are usually tan, buff, gray, or brown when fired. They are used for cooking wares and decorative pottery.

SYNTHETIC OR COMPOUNDED CLAYS

Many clay bodies are compounded in the laboratory through experimental blends of various materials. Bodies are compounded to make them suitable to different types of ware—to make them more or less plastic, to make them vitrify at certain temperatures, and to control porosity. As a potter you will have to choose a compounded clay body suitable to your uses.

TYPES OF CLAY

When you shop for clay, you may hear the many varieties called by names that are sometimes confusing at first. The most common classifications are earthenware, stoneware, and porcelain clays. Classification is based on the nature of the clay and not on the finished appearance of the products made from each type of clay. The following paragraphs describe the characteristics of these clays separately:

Earthenware. Natural clay bodies coming under this heading are red or brown when fired to maturity. Maturing range is usually between 1800 and 2100 degrees F. Compounded earthenware bodies may be any color—red, brown, tan, buff, white, or cream—and may require temperatures as high as 2300 degrees F. for maturing.

Some characteristics of earthenware are: comparatively coarse grain structure, low chipping resistance in finished ware, and deformation of the ware if fired to point of vitrification of the clay body. When a fragment of earthenware which has been fired to maturity is examined under the microscope, it can be seen that the grains in the body structure retain their individual characteristics. Only partial vitrification has taken place, and single clay particles can be pushed from the mass with a hard steel point.

Earthenware products should be rather thick-

Stoneware is fine-textured but sturdy, vitrifies at high temperatures.

Earthenware is coarse-grained, thick-walled, easiest for beginning potter.

21

Mixed media sculptural form shows applied and modeled areas as well as the use of string and clay beads. The form was paddled before holes were pierced and modeled areas were applied. Michael O'Donnell

walled and simply formed for straightforward unsophisticated effects. It is wise for beginners to choose an earthenware body because this material is well suited to the kind of ware made while skills are developing.

Stoneware. This may be either a natural or compounded body. It is more refined than earthenware, is usually buff, tan, or gray when fired, and in most instances matures satisfactorily at temperatures from 2100 to 2300 degrees F. The grain structure of stoneware is finer than that of earthenware clay; products made from it have greater resistance to chipping, and the strength of the material makes it suitable for kitchen and baking ware. Microscopic examination of a broken fragment of fired ware will show loss of identity grains, a greater degree of vitrification than seen in the earthenware shard, and it will not be possible to separate any single grain from the mass with a steel point.

Products made from this material should have walls of medium thickness and be more refined in form than those made of earthenware.

Porcelain. This is the aristocrat of clay bodies—the most highly refined of all clay body types. It is rarely found as a natural body but is compounded as a blend of kaolins, china clays, ball clays, and feldspars. Characteristic properties are: extreme fineness of grain structure, hardness and toughness when fired, resistance to acids, translucence, and complete vitrification when fired to maturity. Color is usually white or blue-white when fired, and maturing temperatures are between 2250 and 2500 degrees F., depending on body composition. Examination of a broken fired fragment shows that the whole mass vitrifies to resemble glass; no particles can be seen separately or removed, and the material will not scratch under a steel point.

Porcelain pieces may be either thin-walled and delicate or rugged and massive. Regardless of the wall thickness, porcelain pieces should be refined in line and sophisticated in shape.

Products made of any of these types of clay described will vary in quality according to the potter's skill, ability, and understanding of his materials. Complete understanding of the possibilities and potentialities of any clay body will come only through actual working experience with it.

Earthenware, stoneware, and porcelain bodies are available from ceramic supply houses (see Suppliers List).

LOW-FIRE PORCELAIN

Bodies which become vitreous at low temperatures may be called low-fire porcelain, synthetic porcelain, or soft-paste porcelain. Owing to their high content of flux (glass-forming material), they become very soft at maturing temperature. When being fired they should be supported evenly on a tile coated with kiln wash rather than on stilts or pins. Since they may contain less clay than other bodies, bentonite is sometimes used to increase plasticity. Low-fire porcelain bodies should be used to make small pieces and ornaments, since large pieces may slump when fired. The following are compositions for two low-fire porcelain bodies that you can prepare yourself.

Cone 07-05 Body

English china clay	20 pbw
Kentucky special ball clay	23
Cullet (powdered glass)	22
Kona A3 feldspar	35
Bentonite	3

Screen dry, add 60% water, mix thoroughly by hand, dry on a plaster bat, and wedge for use.

Nephelene Syenite Body (becomes vitreous and translucent at cone 3)

Nephelene syenite	55 pbw
Kentucky ball clay	10
Edgar plastic kaolin	25
Flint	10
Bentonite, 2% to 3% addition	

To avoid lumps, screen bentonite with other materials before adding water.

SELF-GLAZING BODY (Egyptian Paste)

A self-glazing body contains a soluble substance which crystallizes on the surface of the piece as it dries and melts into a glaze when fired. The body must contain enough frit or cullet to act as a flux and tighten the pores of the clay. It must have enough soluble crystalline material to settle on the surface and form a coating of glaze, and it must contain enough clay to permit forming. In addition, it should contain enough flint to prevent crazing. Such a body is called Egyptian paste because of its use by ancient Egyptian potters.

If you try one of the self-glazing bodies listed in this section, remember that the glaze crystallizes

Japanese Raku ware tea bowl made in 1790 is typical of present-day Raku bowls.

Raku bowl, pinch-formed. Outside bottom half is black, inside and top half is brown. Beatrice Wax

on the surface of the ware as it dries, so do not scrape the piece, and trim only enough to form the foot. Mix the coloring oxide with the body before adding water. Since the paste may be difficult to manipulate on the wheel, only small forms should be attempted.

The following body, developed by Cecile McCann, can be thrown and will have a turquoise glaze when 2% copper carbonate is added, a purple glaze when 1% manganese carbonate is added, and a strong yellow-green glaze when 1% lead chromate is added:

Self-Glazing Body (cone 06)

Powdered flint	35 pbw
Cullet	20
Kentucky ball clay #4	23
Crystalline soda or soda ash	4
Bentonite	3

Another self-glazing body, which fires turquoise mottled with black areas and has a surface texture similar to that of Egyptian scarabs, and which can also be thrown for small forms, was developed by Arthur Baggs:

Egyptian Paste (cone 07)

Ivory Fat ball clay	27 pbw
Nephelene Syenite	20
Flint	35
SS-65 powdered (Cal Quartz)	5
Soda ash	7
Copper carbonate	3

Prepare self-glazing bodies by screening all materials together, then add water until mixture is consistency of cream and hand-grind thoroughly in mortar. Permit body to air dry until it can be hand-wedged and thrown. When leather-hard, trim foot, dry, set level and flat in kiln on slabs of porous fire brick coated with kiln wash, and fire.

RAKU WARE

Japanese raku ware has been made for centuries and is a special favorite with tea ceremony devotees. The body for raku ware is a high-fire plastic fire clay mixed with fine grog or sand. Traditionally, raku ware is made *tebineri* (without the use of the wheel). Forms such as tea bowls should be pinch-formed or coil-built with walls ½" to ⅜" thick. After forming, the ware is biscuited at a low temperature (about 1800 degrees F.), a lead glaze is brushed on, and the ware is fired again until the glaze is melted. As soon as the glaze is melted, the ware is removed from the kiln with tongs. The soft underfired body and removal from the kiln while red-hot assure a crazed glaze. The Japanese say such a combination will not cause a harsh discordant sound when the tea is whisked.

A Raku Body (biscuit fire at cone 07)

Lincoln fire clay	70 pbw
Fine grog	30

The body of the raku bowl shown is sculpture clay mixed with sand. The piece was pinch-formed and biscuited, the outside bottom half was coated with black glaze, and the inside and top half of the outside were coated with brown glaze. As soon as the glaze melted, the piece was removed from the kiln with tongs, cooled in sawdust, then dipped in a bucket of water.

Black Raku Glaze

Frit #3110	20 pbw
White lead	60
Flint	20
Black stain	2
Cobalt carbonate	1
GMC gum powder	1

Brown Raku Glaze

Frit #3396	60
Cullet	20
White lead	20
GMC gum powder	1

MIXED MEDIA

Within the last ten to fifteen years, we have gone through a number of movements in the ceramics field. At the present time, these seem to have more or less run their course. This is particularly true in the fields of urinals and toilet bowls, funk art, and the "happening," in which unfired clay objects are washed away by fountains, dropped into lakes, or splattered on the frozen surfaces of lakes. These ideas are all very exciting, and some are quite original. One of the movements that seems to have survived in the area of sculpture is that of mixed media.

Among the mixed media are three or four types that seem to endure year after year. One that has become very common is the use of paint or lacquer on both fired and unfired clay objects. There is also the combination of fired clay forms and leather, wood, string, or wire. Tanned deerskin is the ideal material to combine with clay. The piece should be made with raised, modeled areas; these will be covered with leather after the piece is fired. The piece is coated with a glaze that provides the desired contrast with the leather. After the piece is glost fired, the leather should be cut to fit the designated area exactly, and the edges should be skived to a paper thin, tapered edge. The modeled area should then be coated with epoxy resin glue and the leather pressed and smoothed into place.

If string is used to suspend the piece, the holes should be cleanly drilled or punched into the piece when it is leather-hard. The string can then be slipped through and epoxied into place when the piece is finished. If the piece is to be glazed, care should be taken not to fill the holes while glazing. If some glaze should get into the holes, it should be cleaned out with a wet cloth wound around a matchstick.

There are many more mixed media combinations possible—just use your imagination. For example, many interesting things have been done with clay and feathers, as well as with styrofoam and clay combinations.

This mixed media sculpture, entitled "Family Tree," consists of slab boxes and wood. Grog and vermiculite were incorporated into the clay and coffee grounds were pressed into the man's face; iron oxide and porcelain slip complete the decoration. Betty Cornell

3
Preliminary
Steps

The basic steps to be followed in the handling of clay are the same regardless of the kind of clay used or the purpose for which it is intended.

MIXING POWDERED CLAY

Clay purchased in powder form is mixed with water to make it a plastic mass. To mix, fill a large dishpan or small tub about one-third full of water. Sift the clay over the water, one handful at a time, until the clay settles on top of the water to make a coating about 1" thick. Cover the pan with paper or cloth and let the unstirred mixture set overnight. On the following day mix and stir it thoroughly. If the mass is too thick to knead, add more water; if too thin, add dry clay. The clay can be stored when it is soft and pliable but does not stick to the hands. Since clay improves with aging in a damp condition, mix it as far ahead of time of use as you can. Wrap the clay in damp cloth and store in a covered crock for at least one week before using.

RECONDITIONING CLAY

Scraps of dry clay and broken ware that was not fired can be reclaimed and re-used. Spread the lumps and scraps out on a hard surface and pound them with a mallet or piece of wood used paddle-fashion until the largest remaining pieces are about the size of a walnut. Put the reclaimed clay into a large pan and cover with water, allowing an excess of about 1" above the top of the clay. Permit the clay to soak without stirring for at least twelve

hours. If by that time the clay has soaked up all the water, cover with water once more and let it set an additional six hours. Then stir thoroughly, breaking any remaining lumps with your hands, and add dry powdered clay slowly until it can be kneaded into a mass of the proper consistency.

If you have no powdered clay, ladle the reclaimed clay onto a large, dry plaster bat. Turn it over as soon as it can be handled, watching to see that the clay does not get too dry. When putty-like, knead it thoroughly and store. Any clay too wet to work can be conditioned by kneading it on a dry plaster bat.

If the clay becomes too stiff in the crock, despite the damp cloths, it can usually be reconditioned by punching holes in it and filling the holes with water, then covering the whole mass with a saturated cloth. Let the clay set for a day or so and then take it from the crock and rework it.

Clay will not deteriorate or suffer from neglect even if left in the crock for long periods. It may mold, but this will not hurt it. To be kept workable over long periods, however, it should have extra cloth wrappings—turkish toweling is excellent—and the wrappings should be sprinkled with water occasionally.

WEDGING

When a portion of the clay is taken from the crock to be shaped, it must first be wedged. This is the process which is employed to force any air bubbles from the mass and to make it uniform in texture thorughout. Bubbles, or "blebs" as they are

Properly wedged, the clay ball is smooth and free of air pockets.

sometimes called, will not cause clay products to explode in the kiln as is popularly believed, but they will cause the piece to crack during either drying or firing. A bubble in the wall of a piece being thrown is particularly annoying.

To wedge your clay, first roll and pat it into a flat rectangular mass. Cut this in two by slicing it with the length of piano wire held taut in the hands, or by bringing it down over a wire stretched between two upright pieces of wood fastened to opposite edges of the table. Slap the two pieces together smartly on the tabletop with the cut edges out. Reshape the rectangle, cut it in two with wire, and again slam the pieces on table, one on top of the other with cut ends out. Repeat until the wire-cut surfaces show the inside of the mass to be free from holes and of a smooth and even texture throughout.

Wedging clay is sometimes compared to kneading bread dough. In reality they are opposing processes, in that wedging is done to eliminate air

from the mass and dough is kneaded to incorporate air into it. Slap and smack the clay mass with the palms of your hands—rather than folding and punching it with your knuckles or the tips of your fingers thereby making air-catching holes.

When a project is complete, rewedge the remaining clay, shape it into a ball, and wrap it for storage in the crock. Clay used for practice throwing on the wheel should also be rewedged before being returned to storage. As the clay used in this manner will probably be too wet for immediate wedging, place it on a plaster bat until it is dry enough to handle.

MAKING PLASTER BATS

The plaster-topped wedging table and bats of various shapes and sizes are indispensable to the potter who works with clay in considerable amounts. The following are directions for mixing plaster and pouring bats.

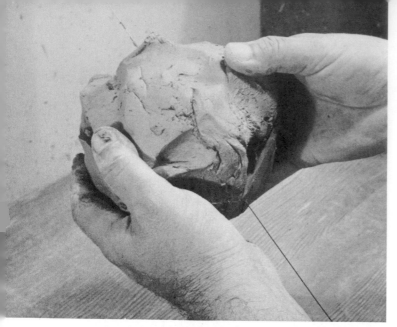

Slice ball of clay with piano wire.

Split ball shows air pockets.

To make a plaster bat you will need potter's plaster purchased from your ceramic supply house, water, a mixing pan, and a form of the size and shape desired for the bat. A cardboard box will make a form for the square or rectangular bat; a cake or pie tin will do for the round one. The form need not be strong or durable, but it must be leakproof or the plaster will flow out while still liquid. Seal any cracks or broken corners in your paper-box form by smoothing clay coils over the inside of the box. The box can be torn away after the plaster has hardened. Paper pie plates can be used in the same way.

If metal pie plates are to be used, oil them lightly before filling with plaster. To simplify removing the bat from a straight-sided metal cake pan, line the sides with a coating of clay ½" thick. When the plaster is set, the clay liner can be dug out with the wooden modeling tool and the bat dislodged easily by tapping the bottom of the pan.

Pie-size bats should be at least 1" thick, because plaster is brittle and thin sections are easily broken. Larger bats are best made 2" or 3" thick, and the wedging tabletop may be 5" or 6" thick.

SOME APPROXIMATE PROPORTIONS FOR BATS

To make plaster bats in a variety of sizes, you will need the following approximate quantities of ingredients:

4" × 4"	11 oz. plaster to ½ pint water
6" × 6"	1 lb., 6 oz. plaster to 1 pint water
5" × 10"	2 lbs., 12 oz. plaster to 1 quart water
9" × 10"	4 lbs., 2 oz. plaster to 3 pints water
10" × 10"	5 lbs., 8 oz. plaster to 2 quarts water

To mix plaster in larger amounts, use the following proportions:

6 lbs., 14 oz. plaster to 2½ quarts water

8 lbs., 4 oz. plaster to 3 quarts water

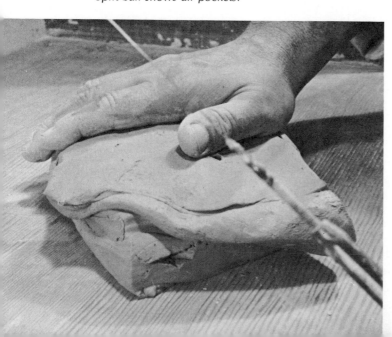

Clay is slammed on table to drive air out of ball, make it pliable.

11 lbs. plaster to 4 quarts water

13 lbs., 8 oz. plaster to 5 quarts water

16 lbs., 8 oz. plaster to 6 quarts water

To estimate the amount of liquid plaster needed to fill a form, first establish the volume of water required to fill it, and allow a little extra. The entire form should be filled with one batch of plaster, as layers of plaster do not always join well and a bat made in two pours may split.

To mix the plaster, first put the required amount of water in the mixing bowl. Sift the dry plaster powder through your fingers, one handful at a time, onto the water in the center of the bowl. Continue to add plaster without stirring or shaking the mixture until it stands in a cone 1½" to 2" above the water at the bowl's center. Wait until the cone has absorbed enough water to wet it through —this usually takes one or two minutes—then immerse your hand in the mixture and stir gently around and around until the plaster mix coats your hand like a glove. Avoid splashy, vigorous movements while stirring plaster as these result in the incorporation of unwanted air in the mix.

When the mixture forms a creamy coating over your hand it is ready to pour. Put the form on a level surface and fill it smoothly and quickly, again without splashing. Plaster sets quickly; it goes through a heating process as it hardens, and as soon as it has heated and cooled it will be stiff enough to remove from the form. However, it is best to wait about thirty minutes after pouring before removal. Scrape the edges of the fresh bat with a knife to remove any sharp fins or chips, and give them a final smoothing with a damp paper towel before setting the bat away to dry completely.

An immediate clean-up after pouring plaster is important. Wipe the plaster from the mixing bowl with disposable paper towels or crumpled newspaper. Wash any remaining plaster from the bowl and pour this water, as well as the water used to rinse your hands, outside. Never pour plaster rinsings in plumbing drains as it will clog them.

PLASTER BAT. 1. Sift plaster onto water by handfuls.

2. Pour plaster into form smoothly and quickly.

3. Scrape sharp fins and chips from edges of bat.

Hippopotamus made by pinch-modeled technique shows delightful possibilities of this method.

4
The Pinch
Method

When you pinch a pottery form from a ball of plastic clay, you are following a method practiced by potters for thousands of years. Oriental craftsmen in particular have found it a way to produce beautiful forms, and some of the most highly prized bowls used in the Japanese tea ceremonies were made by pinching.

Making a pinched pot is an excellent manner in which to become acquainted with the properties of clay. Pots made in this way should be small but they can nevertheless fill many uses. Pinch pots serve as individual nut or candy bowls, relish dishes, ash trays, match holders, and as the small dish called a "spoon drip," which is used on the stove for receiving the stirring spoon.

Clay used to make the pinched form should be fine-grained and plastic, free from grog or coarse sand particles.

"HANDY" ASH TRAY

A convenient ash tray which fits the hand is made as follows. Cut a piece about the size of a golf ball from a wedged mass of clay and roll and pat it round. Support the clay ball on the palm of your left hand and apply downward pressure in the exact top center of the ball with the thumb of your right hand. Bring the fingers of your right hand against the outside surface of the ball in a pinching motion. While pinching the clay with the right hand, lift and shift it slightly, turning the ball one finger-width in a counterclockwise direction. Bring the right hand back the width of one finger and repeat this step. You will find as you work that

the thumb gradually sinks into the clay ball and that the wall between the thumb and fingers thins and expands.

As the form expands, pinch the bottom of the piece between the end of the thumb and middle finger of your right hand until the bottom is about ¼" thick. If edges show signs of cracking, moisten lightly with a sponge and gently rub the rim to close cracks. Thin out the walls by pinching until they are of a uniform thickness of about ¼".

To give the ash tray its free form, hold the bowl loosely in the left hand. Slowly close the hand to gently squeeze to shape as desired. Set the tray on a flat surface to flatten the bottom, and the piece may then be set away to dry for future firing.

THE PINCHED BOWL

Though the procedure for making the pinched bowl is related to that for the handy ash tray, they are not identical. For this project more clay is used and you will work with both hands while the clay rests on a paper which permits it to move freely on the tabletop.

The pinched bowl shown above is useful as a cereal, grapefruit, nut, or candy bowl. To make it, you will need about 1½ pounds of clay. If you have no scales or means of weighing the clay, use a piece about the size of a regulation baseball. You should have a piece of folded newspaper or paper towel to permit the clay to move freely on the tabletop.

Pat the clay into a ball and place the ball of clay on the paper. Place the tips of both thumbs on top

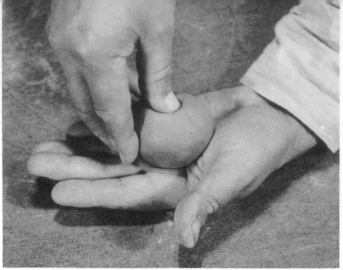
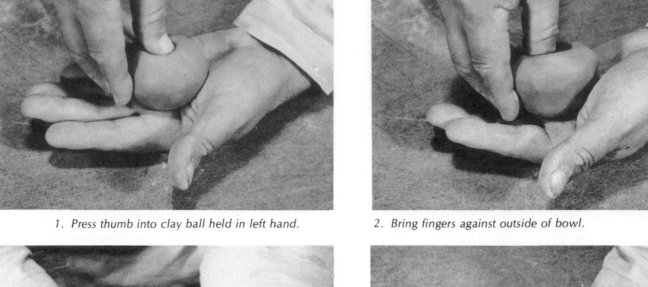

1. Press thumb into clay ball held in left hand.

2. Bring fingers against outside of bowl.

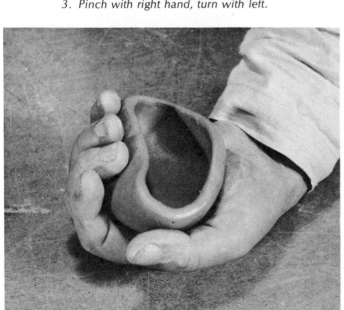

3. Pinch with right hand, turn with left.

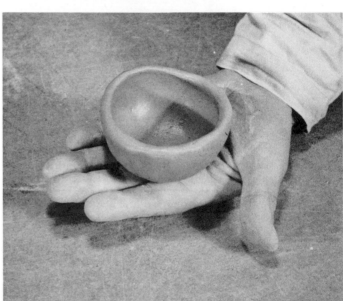

4. Thin out walls to uniform ¼" thickness.

5. Slowly close hand to squeeze to shape.

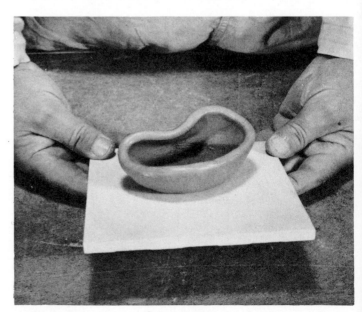

6. Set on flat surface to flatten bottom.

of the clay ball as close to the exact center as possible. Press downward lightly with the thumbs and exert a mild pinching pressure between the thumbs and fingers of both hands. As you pinch the clay, turn it one finger-width in a clockwise motion. Repeat the operation until there is ½" of clay between the ends of your thumbs and the paper. The ball of clay will expand until you have a hole about 2" in diameter in the center of the clay ball. Continue pinching and spreading the ball until you have a bowl of the size and shape you wish.

THE ALL-PURPOSE DISH

The asymmetrical pottery forms shown above are all-purpose dishes particularly useful on the dinner or luncheon table. They can be made with any desired variation in form. They can be made in any size you wish, though when flat forms such as this are too large, they often warp (twist) during drying or firing.

To make a piece like those above, you will need a piece of medium plastic clay about the size of a large cucumber. Pat the coil between the hands, then pinch it until it is uniformly about ⅜" in thickness. The resulting pancake will be somewhat larger than your right hand, and a somewhat irregular rectangle in shape. Support the clay pancake on the palm of your left hand or place it on a paper on the table top, and gently pinch the edge between the thumb and the fingers of your right hand with the thumb on the upper and the fingers against the lower side of the pancake. As you pinch the clay, gently turn the edge upward. Work all the way around the pancake, using the same amount of pressure each time you pinch the edge. Uniformity of pressure insures uniformity of wall thickness. Avoid sharp angles or corners either on the inside or outside for greater ease in glazing and later in washing after use.

THE PINCH-MODELED FIGURE

Making a small pinch-modeled figure offers an excellent opportunity for the development of the creative imagination in both children and adults. Children not only enjoy this method of making small figures, but they often show more ability at the start than adults.

Figures made in this way should be small. Start

Suggested shapes for pinch pots.

33

Pinched bowl formed from orange-sized ball of clay has glazed foot-ring. Harold Driscoll

Asymmetrical dishes are easily pinched from hand-sized slab of clay.

with a portion of wedged clay of medium-soft consistency about the size and shape of a cheese-spread glass. Grasp this elongated cylinder in the right hand and squeeze. While still holding the clay, strike one end of the wad lightly on the table top to flatten it.

Set the flattened end of the wad on a tile, plaster bat, or bench whirler so that the work can be readily turned and seen from all sides during the modeling.

Examine the squeezed clay for suggestions of form or figure and add any details needed to enhance it. Ears can be pinched to shape, eyes developed by pinching bits from the mass, and parts of the shape accented with finger modeling. Delicacy of detail is neither desirable nor necessary in this type of figure, and its charm will be its simplicity. Let your fingers be your only modeling tools, and remove none of the clay from the original cylinder if you want to achieve the most direct effects.

When modeling of the figure is complete, let it dry very slowly and completely before firing.

THE COMBINED PINCHED FORM

Practice making pinch bowls of various sizes. You'll find that with practice each one will be better than the last. When you have mastered uniform wall thickness and control of form you are ready to combine two pinch bowls to make a closed form, such as two half-spheres to make a hollow sphere, or two half egg shapes to make an ovoid. Or you can make a bottle such as that shown in the nearby photographs.

To make a bottle, start with two well-wedged balls of clay of the same size. Pinch each ball into a good-sized bowl shaped like half an egg. Check the diameter and wall thickness of both bowls with calipers and ruler to be sure they are consistent. The inside of a bottle is hard to clean, so smooth the inside surface of both bowls by pressing it with a large, smooth pebble. To insure a solid joint later, smooth and carefully level the rims. Place the bowls rim down on a smooth level surface and set them aside to become leather-hard. When they are hard enough to handle without losing their shape, score the rims of both bowls with the tip of your fettling knife. Coat the scored surfaces with slip, and press the bowls solidly together, being careful not to distort them. Use the tip of your modeling tool to press the clay firmly toward the joint on both sides, while at the same time deeply scoring the surface. Now roll out a

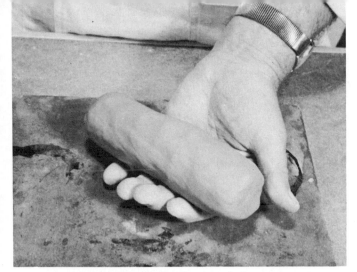

1. Start with cylinder of wedged clay.

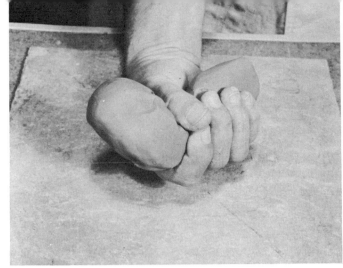

2. Squeeze clay cylinder.

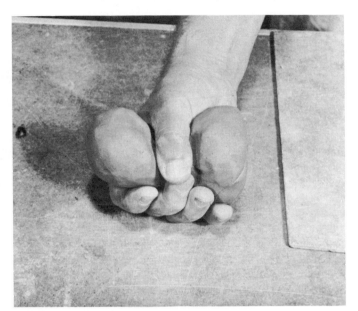

3. Flatten one end for base.

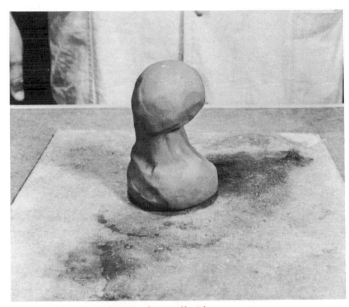

4. Set clay on end, view from all sides.

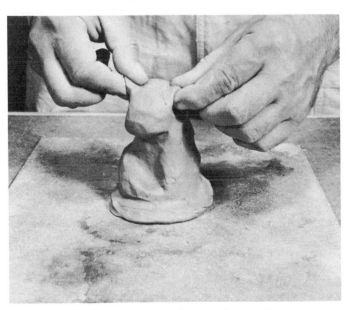

5. Let fingers be the only modeling tools.

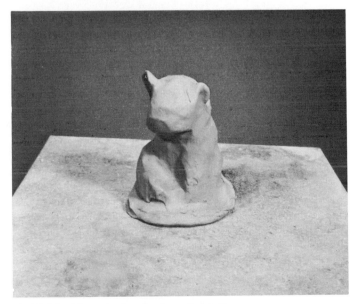

6. Finished form is simple, free of detail.

coil ½″ in diameter. Coat the scored surface of the sphere with slip, place the coil in position on the joint, and press it firmly into place. Weld the coil in both directions from the joint, then paddle the coil to follow the contour of the form. Paddle one end of the form to make a flattened base. Cut a hole in the other end, and score the surface around hole.

Pinch a neck from a small ball of clay and flare one end of it for a lip. Score the unflared end, add slip to the scored surfaces of the neck and bowl, and attach them. When the piece is leather-hard, carve the decoration.

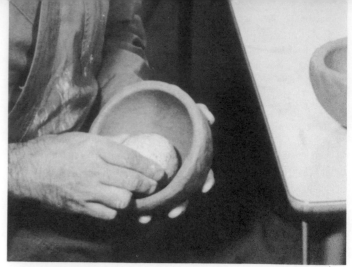

1. Smooth inside of bowl with a pebble.

4. Add slip and place coil on top of joint.

7. Paddle coil to contour of form.

2. Measure wall thickness with a ruler.

3. Press clay toward joint, scoring surface.

5. Press coil firmly into place.

6. Weld coil in both directions from joint.

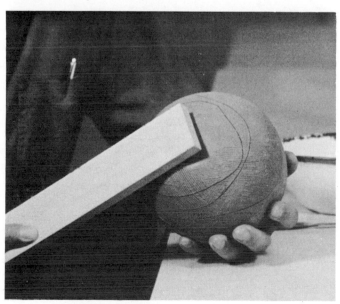

8. Paddle one end of form for base.

9. Attach neck with slip and weld.

Large stoneware bottle shows subtle and pleasing non-symmetry natural to large coil-built pieces. Robert Bolger

5
Building
with Coils

Building forms with clay coils is one of the easiest and most rewarding ways of making pottery. This method permits the beginner to make pieces in any desired shape and size and allows the experienced craftsman to develop forms not readily achieved by other means.

Almost any clay can be used for coil building. It should be plastic but moderately stiff to allow the coils to be lifted without undue stretching or loss of shape.

Possibilities of form in coil-built ware are unlimited. Make your coiled pieces round, oval, rectangular, or in irregular shapes. Your products can be bowls, vases, jugs, pitchers, cannisters, or lamp bases, to name but a few of the possibilities. Many of these can be built as coiled cylinders, others as expanding coiled forms. Procedures used in making both follow.

THE COILED CYLINDER

Begin with three to four pounds of wedged clay. Take a small portion of it and pat it into a ball. Place the ball on an unglazed tile or partially saturated plaster bat, using a bench whirler if one is available. Pat the ball to make a pancake of uniform thickness. Base thickness varies according to the planned dimensions of the finished piece. A pot 3" in diameter will ordinarily have a base about ⅜" thick; one 6" will have a base about ½" thick; the pot 9" in diameter will have a base about ¾" thick, etc.

Use a compass or dividers to outline the shape of the circular base. Cut through the clay along the outline, holding the knife vertically, and remove the excess clay.

To make the coils which will form the wall of the pot, first make cigar-shaped wads of clay. Roll these under your fingers on a damp, but not wet, tabletop. Spread out the fingers of both hands, resting them lightly on the clay. As you roll it forward under your spread fingers, also move your hands outward to lengthen coil. Roll the coil forward for a distance of about 12", then roll it back again. Repeat until the coil is made. If the clay is stiff or develops cracks, the tabletop may be too dry. If it sticks, the tabletop is too wet or the clay is too soft. Hard pressing on the coil will flatten it or make sections of varying diameters. Try to make it a smooth, even rod.

Coils should be about as big around as a lead pencil for a piece 3" in diameter. Larger pieces will use larger coils: the 6" cylinder calls for coils ⅜", the 9" diameter for ½" coils, etc.

Place the first coil around the entire top edge of the base so that it is directly above the edge. Cut off the excess coil. Press the ends of the coil firmly together and weld the joint by dragging a bit of the clay from one end of the coil across the other. Weld the joint all around the edge. Use the first finger of your right hand to press the first coil firmly against the base as you support it with the fingers of your left hand. Weld the coil to the base both inside and out by dragging small amounts of clay from the coil across the joint to seal it completely.

Place each additional coil squarely on top of the one below it, welding ends and joints between coils on both inside and outside of the piece as you

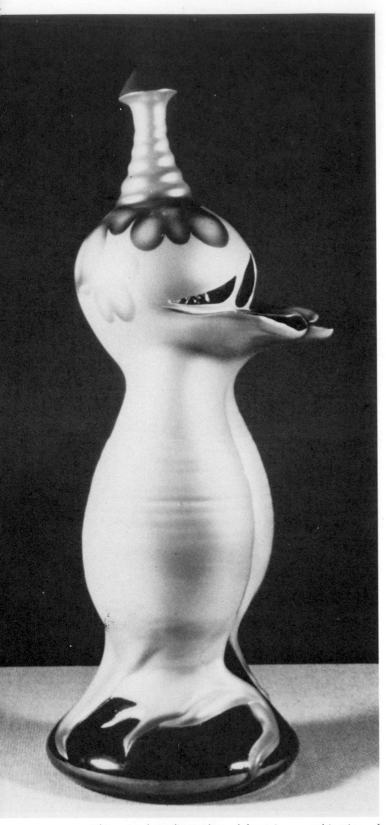

This mixed media sculptural form is a combination of thrown and coil-built parts. Lacquer was used instead of glaze to create a finished surface decoration. Shigeru Miyamoto

build. Be sure to place the ends of the coil at different locations in the wall each time.

If coils are added too rapidly, the wall of the piece will sag. To prevent this, allow the coils to stiffen slightly before adding new ones. A strong union between coils is essential, however, so moist clay must not be added to any that has become rigid. If the top coil becomes stiff, chop light serrations in it with the knife, wrap it with a wet cloth, and allow it to stand until the clay rim has regained plasticity. Then continue to add coils until the piece is of the desired height.

THE COILED EXPANDING FORM

Prepare the base and make the coils as for the straight-sided cylinder. To make this form expand outward, make the coil slightly longer and place each successive coil toward the outer edge of the preceding one. To draw the form inward, place added coils toward the inner edges of preceding ones. Weld ends and joints as previously described.

When the wall weight extends beyond the base, the form tends to sag unless the lower coils are allowed to stiffen slightly. Work on several pieces at once or allow the single project to set in warm air for a short period until it stiffens slightly before adding coils.

USING TEMPLATES

To control the shape of a coil-built form, you will need to use a cardboard guide known as a "template." This guide, which you can easily make yourself, is helpful in forming large pieces such as vases and bottles; its use is mandatory in making matching pieces such as a pair of lamp bases or a set of mugs.

To make a template, first select the desired shape. Then, using graph paper (available from stationery stores), draw the outline of the shape. To enlarge the shape once it is drawn, count the squares covered by any part of it and draw an equal number of larger squares on paper. Draw the profile outline in the large squares exactly as you see it in the small ones, using same number of squares.

A template insures symmetry. Coil-built asymmetrical forms are made without the use of a template, so careful planning before building is necessary. Some preliminary sketches of the form to be made may help in the planning. Construction of an asymmetrical form is the same as that of other coil-built forms. It is also possible to start out building a symmetrical form and then alter its symmetry in various ways before it has become leather-hard by pressing the wall with the hand from the inside or from the outside. Both inside and outside pressures can also be used. The symmetry of a form can also be changed by paddling the surface in various ways.

To make a template, cut out the form, fold it down the center, and transfer the folded pattern to a cardboard rectangle large enough to accommodate it. Position the bottom of the half-shape in the lower left corner of the cardboard. The bottom edge of the cardboard rectangle should be flush with the fold. Cut along the pattern outline with a sharp knife or a single-edge razor blade. The cardboard with the proposed pot shape cut away is your template.

Use the template by placing it beside the coiled shape as coils are added. Check around the piece frequently to be sure you are not stretching the coils. Do not use the template as a scraper.

SURFACE TEXTURES

In forming the coiled pot you will find that you can smooth one coil into the next to make a surface of a uniform pebbled texture, or allow each to remain rounded to produce a ribbed, corrugated effect. The smoothed coils can be smoothed still further by rubbing them with a shiny, hard pebble or the bowl of a kitchen spoon. Do not use sandpaper or steel wool, as these will affect the glaze. Combine the corrugated, finger-smoothed or polished surfaces for interesting variations in texture in your coiled pieces.

LARGE COIL-BUILT FORMS

Once you have mastered the fundamentals of coil building, you are ready to build some large forms for use in the garden, on the patio, or by the fireplace. An unusual method for making large coil-built forms is the paddle and anvil technique used by the southeastern American Indians hundreds of years ago. To use this process you will need a good-sized anvil over which to form the ware. The Indians used a boulder shaped somewhat like a large ice cream cone resting on its rim, with a broad and somewhat flattened or rounded point.

If you cannot find such a boulder, cast a large, solid block of plaster, then carve, scrape, file, and sand it until you have an appropriate cone-shaped

Coil construction may be left exposed, as with this bottle; or smoothed over, as with the vase. Ruthadell Horan

hump. A conical anvil shape without any under-cuts is necessary so that the completed clay form can move upward on the anvil as it shrinks while drying, without cracking or splitting.

The shaping paddle should be of sturdy ¾" wood, about 6" to 8" long, and 4" wide, and about a third of its length should be shaped into a handle. All edges of the paddle should be well-rounded to avoid sharp wedge cuts in the clay. A butter paddle may be used, although it is somewhat light in weight for this purpose.

Roll out a number of coils at least 1" in diameter, then keep the coils covered with a damp cloth while working. Drape a piece of burlap smoothly over the anvil, place a thick pancake of clay on top, and paddle it flat. This will be the bottom of the finished piece. Now lap the first coil so that about a third of its thickness covers the edge of the base, and weld it firmly to the outside of the base. Repeat this procedure with successive coils.

Make sure all the coils are pressed solidly together before welding. When you have the coiled piece built to about two-thirds of its final size, start at the base and paddle all around the form, working from the base to the rim. Use the same pressure each time you strike the clay with the paddle to insure uniform wall thickness. The clay will stretch as it is paddled, and the finished form will be a fourth to a third taller than it was before being paddled. When the clay is hard enough to handle, remove the form from the anvil, carefully remove the burlap from the clay (watch out for spots that may stick), finish the foot rim, dry, and fire. If the paddle sticks to the clay surface, it may be carved, wrapped with cord, or covered with cloth. This will prevent sticking and it will also provide a nicely textured surface.

THE STRIKING PROCESS

The Korean and Japanese version of the paddle and anvil technique is called the striking process. In the nearby illustrations, Joe Hysong demonstrates the use of this process to make a large vase form.

For the striking process, the anvil—made of wood, biscuited clay, or plaster—should be smaller than that used previously. It should be the right size to hold comfortably in your hand. It should be shaped like a well-rounded stuffed pillow and should have no sharp edges. The striking implement may be either a wooden mallet with grooves carved into the face to keep it from sticking to the clay, or a paddle as described above.

1. *Measure diameter of base with rule.*

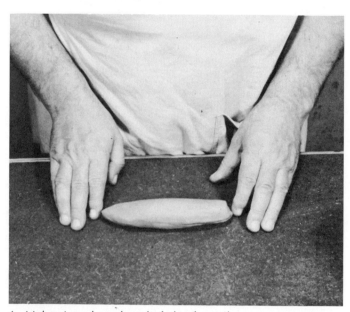

4. *Make cigar-shaped wad of clay for coil.*

7. *Place first coil around top of base.*

2. Cut by turning base, holding knife.

3. Remove excess clay, return it to crock.

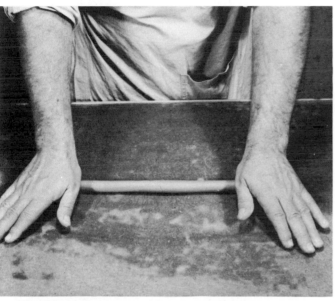

5. Roll back and forth, stretching coil.

6. Try to make smooth, even rod of clay.

8. Weld first coil to base, inside and out.

9. Place subsequent coils directly on top.

Expanding form made by adding larger coils.

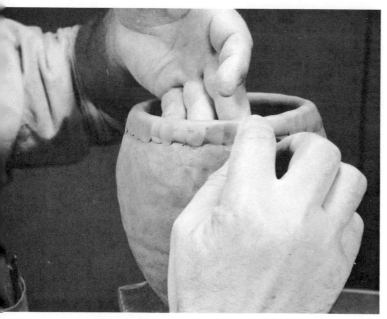

To draw in, place coils on inner edge.

Roughly coil-build about a third of the form, then shape it by supporting the clay on the inside with the anvil as you strike the outside surface with the mallet or paddle. Be sure to move the anvil so it is directly opposite the mallet each time the clay is struck. Also, be sure to cover all the surface of the form.

After shaping, set the form aside for three or four hours to harden. Keep the top coil covered with a damp cloth. As soon as the form will support the weight, build the second third and shape it in the same manner as you did the first third. Be sure to work carefully over the area where the two sections join. After another hardening interval, add the final third and shape it as before. As soon as the form has hardened enough to support the neck, build the neck, attach it, and finish it by hand.

The foot of a large form need not be trimmed, but as soon as such a form can be handled without losing shape, the center portion of the bottom may be pressed inward by hand or it may be repeatedly bumped with the anvil until the bottom is concave. The edge of the concave portion is the foot rim and should be kept level while you are working on the bottom. After you have scraped and sponged any sharp edges, the piece is ready to be dried slowly in a closed box, then fired.

FINISHING TOUCHES

Trim and round the rims of your coiled pieces carefully with the fettling knife and a wet sponge—rounded edges hold a glaze better than sharp edges.

All but the smallest coiled forms should have a foot rim. The foot functions as a protective feature and is an advantage when the piece is glost fired. Wait until the piece is leather-hard to make the foot. Then invert the piece and pencil in a circle on the bottom, making the area between the circle and the rim of the piece match the thickness of the wall. Use a wooden modeling tool and hollow the area within the circle to lower it about ⅛″ for a piece 3″ across, 3/16″ for a piece 6″ across, and ¼″ for a 9″ piece.

Some of your coiled pieces will require lids, handles, or spouts—perhaps all three. These should be made of the same clay and at about the same time as the body of the piece. Attach handles and spouts when the body is leather-hard.

HANDLES

To make a coil handle, use medium-stiff clay and roll a coil of the desired size. Cut it to length and

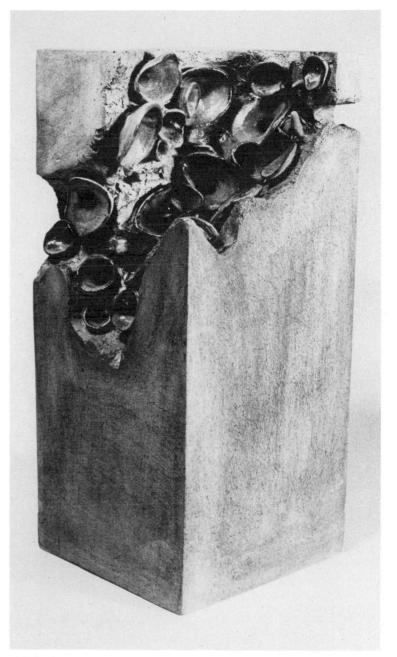

Slab-built stoneware sculpture was first carved when leather-hard, then areas were painted with iron oxide before firing. Robert Bolger

Slab-built stoneware piece illustrates how decoration can be part of the building process. Eileen Fears

1. Build 1/3 of the form, then shape.

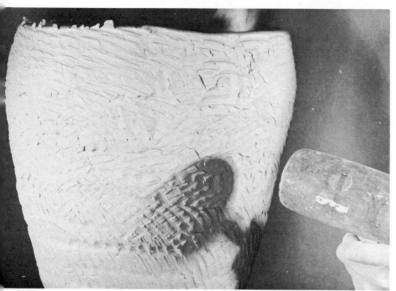

2. Be sure to cover all of the surface.

3. Add the neck and finish by hand.

taper the ends by pinching between thumb and forefinger. Bend and shape it carefully. Scratch the surfaces where the handle will meet the pot and moisten with a paste made of thick clay slip. Press ends in place, weld, and seal joints with added bits of clay for strength.

The pulled handle should be made from relatively stiff clay. Wedge the clay thoroughly and pat it into a pear-shaped wad. Grasp the large end of the wad of clay in the left hand with the small end pointing down. Lubricate the right hand with water and "milk" the small pointed end, pulling it into a long tapered strip of the desired shape and size. Pinch the handle from the wad and appy it to the form; the heavy end is the top of the handle. (Some people prefer to shape it after pulling and permit it to become leather-hard on a plaster bat before attaching it.) Weld it fast and seal the top of both joints with small cigar-shaped fillets of clay.

To make a slab handle, pat a slab of clay slightly thicker than the wall of the container onto the back of an oilcloth. Cut a slab from the pancake the desired width of the handle. Shape and apply the slab to the leather-hard form, sealing the top of each joint with a small cigar-shaped fillet of clay. When the handle is leather-hard, sponge and round all edges.

SPOUTS

Spouts can be made of short coils added directly to the form or built separately and welded in place using the same procedure as that used to attach handles. Then cut the container wall away inside the spout and seal the edges.

The pulled spout is most commonly used on pitchers. The spout should be pulled as soon as the form is completed, while the clay is still plastic. Support the top part of the wall on the outside with the thumb and first finger of the left hand held 1½" to 2" apart. Using the first finger of the right hand, press the clay out between the thumb and finger of the left hand.

The slab spout can best be developed by cutting paper patterns. Select the pattern which is best suited to the form. Roll out or pat out a slab of clay of the desired thickness. Place the pattern on the clay slab and cut through the slab around the edge of the pattern with a fettling knife. Apply the spout to the form as shown in Chapter 9.

Combined pinched forms: Small-neck bottle, paddled vase, bottle with coil neck. Larry Geremone, Gene Chappell, Bill Grossi

Indian burial urn with paddled design, made by paddle and anvil technique. Height 17".

Non-symmetry may be developed by paddling as soon as clay with not stick to paddle. Marvin Wax

COVERS

If your piece is to have a cover, you must first decide if it will be a flanged one and whether it will rest on a rim inside the wall or on top of it. In any case, check the pot rim for roundness as soon as it is completed, pressing it gently with the hands to perfect any irregularities. If the pot is to have an inside lid, first weld a coil inside to form a ledge. The distance from the pot rim to the top of the ledge should equal the wall thickness of the pot. Next, pat out a clay pancake of this same thickness and cut a circle from it equal to the diameter of the pot opening, less ⅛". When the clay circle and pot are both leather-hard, add a modeled knob or coil loop to the lid, sponge it, and fit it to the pot.

To make a cover with a flange, cut a clay circle of same thickness as the pot's wall and equal in size to the outside diameter of pot opening. To locate the position of the flange, subtract the wall thickness plus ¹/16" from the edge of the clay circle. Using dividers, draw this smaller circle on the clay. Make a coil and weld it in position just inside the scribed outline. When both the piece and lid are leather-hard, add a knob to the lid, sponge it, and fit it to the pot.

The outside lid is made by cutting a clay circle

Template useful for controlling large forms, mandatory for matching pieces. Ruthadell Horan

Pitcher with pulled spout, coil handle.

Pitcher with slab spout, pulled handle.

Earthenware teapot with slab spout and pulled handle.

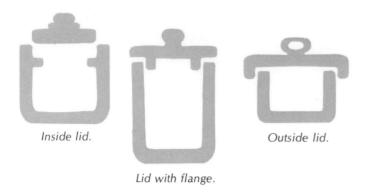

Inside lid.

Lid with flange.

Outside lid.

which is equal in size to the opening diameter of the pot plus twice the wall thickness and an added 3/16". When the clay is cut, add two coils around and on top of the circle as in building a cylinder, welding them firmly in place. Add a knob if desired when the lid and piece are leather-hard. In fitting a lid of this type, allow from 1/8" to 3/16" play between the pot and the lid.

When the shaping of the lid is finished, let the lid and pot dry as separate units. For the best fit, however, biscuit-fire with the lid in place on the pot.

COILED FIGURES

Small but highly decorative figures are easy to make with coils. Try your hand at making a horse like that illustrated nearby, and it will lead you to make other figures of people or animals of your own design.

Start by making a length of coil about 5/8" in diameter. Cut two pieces approximately 4½" long from this and press the pieces together at the center as you hold them parallel. Weld the joint about 1½" long at center to make a solid oval section for the horse's body; the four free ends of the coil will be the legs. Gently bend the section to form an arch and stand it on a tile or plaster bat.

Next, cut a 2¼" coil for the neck. Flatten ½" at one end. Moisten this flat end and an end of the body portion and weld together. In welding parts of figures, joints must be sealed to prevent air from coming between them; air causes them to separate during drying or firing.

The head is made by rolling another 2¼" length of coil to make an egg-shaped ball. Pinch the neck to taper it, and after moistening both the neck end and the large end of the egg shape, weld them together. Make and add eyes and nostrils by rolling and flattening small clay balls about the size of dried peas. A 1" length of coil will make a tail, and two small cigar-shaped wads will make the ears. Add a mane, if you like, made from small clay loops, balls, or buttons.

When all the parts are assembled, the fun of giving the figure expression can begin. Do this while the clay is still plastic and you can arch, bend, or turn neck and head to make your horse look shy, inquisitive, or surprised. At the same time, separate the legs and place the feet in their desired positions.

After the figure has dried and been biscuit-fired, consider glazing it in an imaginative, unhorselike, color. Make it pink, yellow, or blue, for instance, and it will truly be a "horse of a different color."

Horse fashioned from coils can be glazed in imaginative, unhorselike color.

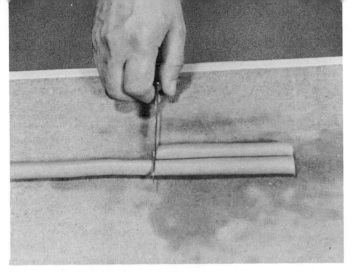

1. Cut two pieces of coil 4½" long.

2. Hold parallel and press center together.

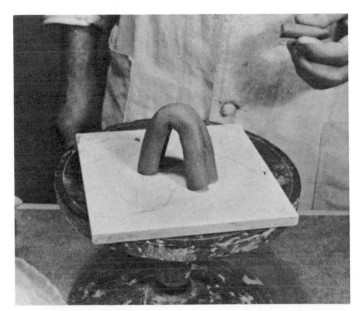

3. Gently bend to form arch, set on bat.

4. Add neck by welding moistened piece of coil.

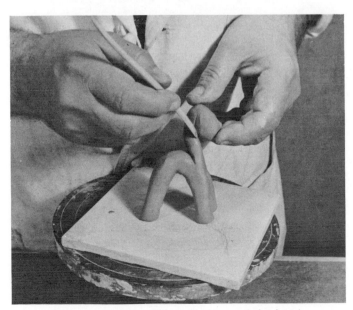

5. Egg-shaped pellet welded to neck for head.

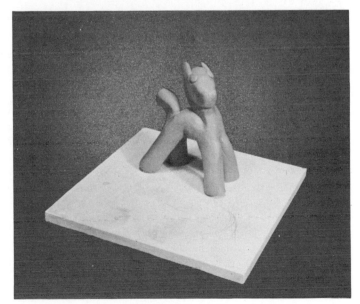

6. With all parts assembled, give personality to horse.

Slab-built stoneware bottle with thrown neck displays decoration impressed into the slab before building. James Lovera

6
Building
with Slabs

Making tiles and constructing forms from flat sheets of clay involve using a pottery technique which has been developed over many centuries. Excavations made in Egypt and Assyria have resulted in finds of tile murals of monumental proportions, and a study of the architecture of Spain, Turkey, and Persia will show a generous use of tiles in these countries.

Almost any clay ware can be used in the making of tiles and slab wares. The fine-grained clays do tend to warp when used in these ways, but they can be improved by the addition of grog (20 to 40 mesh). Earthenware clays with grog added are readily available, or you can add grog to the clay you are using. Add ten or fifteen percent of red grog to white clay to make a good slab-building body—with an interesting speckled effect.

Beginners and experienced potters both enjoy using this method because it makes the forming of geometrically shaped wares a direct and easy process. You can make tiles, boxes with or without lids, flower pots, planters, bowls and straight-sided vases, lamp bases, and innumerable other useful pieces with this simple technique. Cylindrical pieces can also be made with slabs.

MAKING TILES

To make tiles singly or by the dozens, you will need a length of oilcloth to stretch over the worktable, a wooden rolling pin, two guide sticks (about 18" long and as thick as the tiles will be), and a fettling knife.

Put the oilcloth over the table with the cloth side up, and place mass of wedged clay on it. Place wooden guide sticks on two sides of the mass, and roll the clay as you would dough until the whole portion is exactly as thick as the guide sticks.

Mark out squares with a ruler and pencil. These may be any size, but tiles are most often made in 4" or 6" squares. If an exact finished size is important, allow a margin of about ⅛" for shrinkage.

When the tile dimensions are marked and while the clay is still soft, use a fettling knife to cut along the guidelines, penetrating about one-half the thickness of the clay. Make light cuts; do not allow the knife to drag or it will distort the tile edges. These edges will also become distorted if the clay is completely cut through at this stage.

After an hour or two, the clay should stiffen to a cheese-like consistency, and the tile outlines can be cut through completely. Smooth the edges with a wet sponge.

If you are using a grogged clay, the tiles can be dried on an open shelf if turned over every two or three hours during the first day's drying. If the tiles are made of a fine-grained clay which tends to warp, turn them over after sponging the edges and cut grooves in the back to a depth of about one-third of the tile thickness to minimize warping.

Tiles may be dried on a wire screen or sandwiched between 8" plaster bats, but they must lie flat during both the drying and firing periods.

Decorative treatments are frequently used on tiles before they are completely dry. For suggestions about decorating tiles, see Chapter 8.

Slab piece that was paddled after building. Marvin Wax

SLAB PLATES

Making a set of square plates is an interesting project, and the resulting dishes should be an attractive addition to your collection of tableware. Circular plates can also be made from slabs, but they are more difficult to form satisfactorily—the circular form is likely to be irregular, and the flared edge uneven.

Equipment needed is the same as that used in making tiles. In addition, you will need a paper pattern cut to the shape and size of the plate desired.

To make the pattern for the plate illustrated nearby, fold an 8" square of paper in quarters, then fold this square once again. Trim the point to round corners of the square. The finished plate will be smaller than the pattern due to clay shrinkage during drying and firing.

To make a plate, wedge about 1½ pounds of medium-stiff clay and pat it into a ball. Flatten and roll it out with a rolling pin, using guide sticks to make the slab ¼" thick.

Lay the paper pattern on the clay and cut around the pattern outline with a large pin, darning needle, or the point of the fettling knife. Remove excess clay and allow the slab to set until it can be moved without misshaping it.

When stiff enough to handle, move the slab to a plaster bat large enough to support the entire slab. Roll coils ½" in diameter and use these to raise the edges of the slab to give the plate a gently curved rim. Let the plate stand with the edges held up by the supporting coils until it is leather-hard. Then remove the coils and trim the plate edges with knife or a wire-ended modeling tool. Smooth the rim with a wet sponge.

To keep it from warping, the plate should dry slowly. Set it on a damp plaster bat and cover with a damp cloth. Remove the cloth after 24 hours and set the plate away to dry completely before biscuit-firing.

SLAB BOXES

Procedures for rolling slabs to make box forms are the same as those used in making tiles. Patterns of paper or light cardboard will be useful in cutting matching rectangles for sides, ends, etc. Allow cut clay parts to become leather-hard before attempting to build with them.

All joints in the form must be well sealed or they may split during drying or firing. To make good joints, first wet the edges with "slip." Slip, in this case, is a thin cream made of your clay and water. Apply two coats with a soft brush. After pressing the slip-coated joints together, work them solidly into position with a slight rocking motion. If the clay is at all dry, make light scored cuts in the edges before applying slip and joining edges. Joints can be further strengthened and rounded by adding a small coil along inside angles and pressing it along adjoining angles. Seal and weld outside joints with wooden modeling tool. For best results, set the box walls on top of the base, not around it.

When the box is leather-hard, round the edges and outside corners and set it away to dry.

The addition of a well-designed foot and cover will turn a simple box form into an attractive container. To make a foot, invert the box (when it is leather-hard) and add slab strips as shown in the nearby illustrations of making a flared slab bowl.

Lids can be fitted to rest inside the box opening, to rest on top of the box walls, or to cover them. Types of lids are illustrated and described in Chapter 5. Lids for the rectangular box are made by cutting clay rectangles from slabs and fitting them with knobs, flanges, etc.

SLAB BOWL WITH FLARED SIDES

To make a bowl of this type you will need the slab-making equipment previously described and a paper pattern made by folding a rectangle and cutting a narrow, triangular notch from the corner. The bowl pictured is 6" × 7½".

Lay the pattern on a prepared slab of clay and cut around it. Remove excess clay, and when the flat form is stiff enough to lift, score the edges of corner joints by making small incisions along the cut edges with a knife. Work thin slip into the incisions with a soft brush. To make a corner joint, pinch the seams firmly together from the outside. Support the newly formed corner with a brick or a section of wood 2" × 4", then join and support the other corners. Seal corner joints with clay taken from both sides and pushed into the angle with the wooden modeling tool. Cover the completed bowl with a damp cloth and let it set until leather-hard.

As soon as the bowl can be safely handled, invert it and make foot measurements. Mark a line along all four sides of the bottom to act as a guide for positioning the strips which make the foot. Roll out a slab of the same thickness as the bowl—¼" for the bowl shown—and cut four strips ½" wide and approximately the length of the bowl. Cut these to length after they have stiffened.

Decorative tiles call for good design sense. Kenneth Dierck

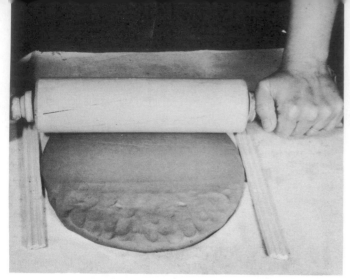

1. Roll out 1½ pounds clay to quarter-inch slab.

2. Cut out clay following paper pattern.

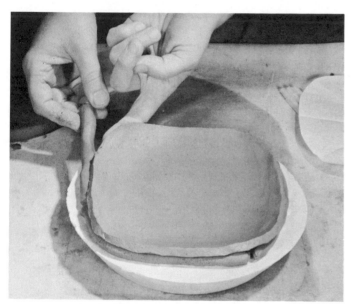

3. Place supporting coil under edge.

4. Trim edges of leather-hard plate with tool.

5. Apply glaze to biscuited plate with brush.

6. Finished, fired plate graces patio table. Paula Palmer

While the strips stiffen, make small incisions in the clay of the bowl bottom just inside the outlines marked for the foot. Next cut the long side pieces to the exact length of the marked area and the short end pieces to a measure ½" shorter than the width of the area. The ends will fit between the sides when joined on the bowl bottom.

To add the foot, first score the edges of the side strips and ½" of inside surface at the ends. Wet the scored edges of these and the matching sections on the bowl bottom with water or thin slip and press together with a slight rocking motion to join securely.

Prepare end strips by scoring one edge and both ends of each and join to bowl in the same manner. Weld all joints solidly on inside and outside. Round inside corners with a modeling tool by drawing a little clay from bowl to strip. At the joint on the inside of the foot, add extra clay by pressing a small coil or "fillet" into adjoining angles.

Set the inverted bowl away in a closed box or cupboard for twelve hours. Moisture in the bowl and foot will equalize in that time and you can then round all the edges with a modeling tool and wet sponge. Be sure to allow the bowl to dry completely before firing.

LARGE SLAB FORMS

When you have discovered the various ways to handle the partially stiffened slabs and the means by which they may be joined together, you are ready to experiment with unusual shapes of larger size. Such large slab forms can follow many patterns and have many variations. Like the smaller forms, they should be carefully planned before you begin to actually work with the clay.

Probably the greatest problems in making large forms, aside from that of actually handling large quantities of clay and keeping it together, is finding sufficient space to roll out the slabs. A patio or garage floor may alleviate this situation. However, if you work on the patio, try to avoid working clay in the hot sun.

The oval drum made by Philip Cornelius (see pages 59, 60) is 28" high overall. For such large slab forms, wall thickness is most important for strength. In this drum, the flat surfaces are ½" slabs separated by a ¾" slab. The assembled drum is 8" wide, 12" high, and 16" long; the supporting base, made from a ¾" slab, is 16" high.

To make the drum, prepare paper patterns for all parts except the pinched spouts. Roll out a ½" slab for the drum faces and a ¾" slab for a separator.

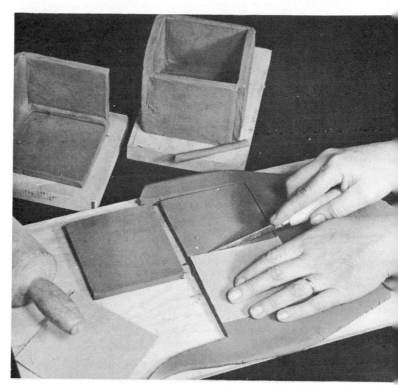

To make sure that box parts will fit, make accurate, squared patterns from cardboard and cut matching clay forms with knife.

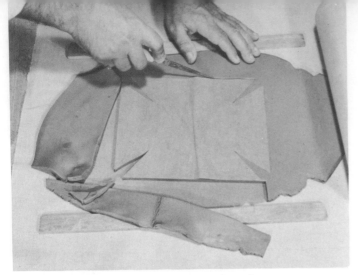

1. Cut around paper pattern, discard excess.

2. Pinch corners together, support with bricks.

3. Attach foot strips to incised lines with slip.

4. Weld foot to bottom with modeling tool.

5. Round leather-hard edges with sponge.

6. Finished piece ready to be biscuit-fired.

Place an oval pattern on the drum face slabs and mark around it with pencil but do not cut the slabs. Set the face slabs and separator aside to harden slightly while you roll out and cut a ¾" slab for the cylindrical base.

Return to the drum and check the slabs for hardness; the ¾" slab should still be plastic but should be able to support itself when stood on edge. Score the face slabs, making incisions ⅛" deep and 1" long with the point of wooden modeling tool inside the pencil-marked ovals. Score all edges of the ¾" separator slab in the same way, and give all scored areas a liberal coating of thick slip. Assemble the separator on one drum face and work it solidly into position with a slight rocking motion. The slip should form a bead both inside and outside the joint. Press the ends of the separator slab solidly together with your thumbs and work them vigorously together with tip of modeling tool. Then reinforce the joint with coils both inside and outside. Weld the coils into position, then paddle flat.

Cut the top drum face from the slab ¼" outside the oval pencil line. Place the top face slab in position and press the joint firmly together until a bead of slip appears entirely around the oval. If a bead does not appear, paddle gently until it does. Permit the drum to harden and assemble the cylindrical base.

As soon as the drum is hardened enough to hold its shape when lifted, paddle the ¼" surplus over the edge of the separator, rounding the edge as you work. Cut through the bottom face slab, leaving ¼" surplus, turn the drum over, and paddle the surplus over the edge as you did on other side. Assemble the drum on the base by cutting the top of base to the contour of drum. Score surfaces to be joined, apply slip, and place drum in position. If base extends beyond drum, lift drum slightly and paddle top of base until it lines up as desired. Press drum firmly into position, and weld solidly to base, reinforcing with clay coil. Invert assembled form and reinforce inside joint also.

Now pinch out a number of varied sizes of small bowls. Select those whose size and shape are most attractive, and mark out their positions on the drum. Cut the bottoms from the bowls, score, add slip, and attach them to the drum separator. A paddle may be used to insure solid joints. Cut through drum separator inside spouts and remove the cutout area. Work all joints firmly together.

An appliqué decoration is optional. If desired, you may use thin slabs; score, slip, and paddle them to the surface. Permit the form to become

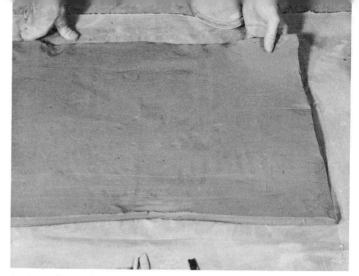

1. Form large slabs on garage or patio floor.

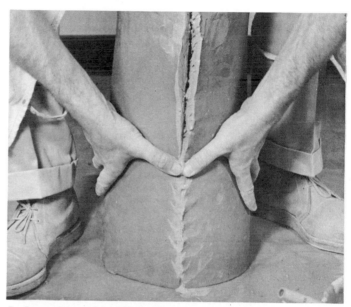

2. Press slab ends solidly with thumbs.

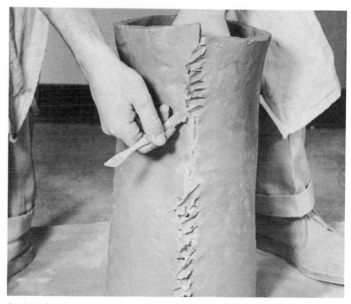

3. Work joint vigorously with modeling tool.

4. Cut top of base to contour of drum.

5. Paddle top of base to line up with drum.

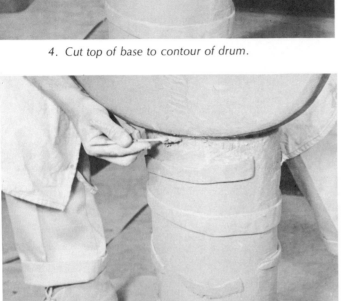

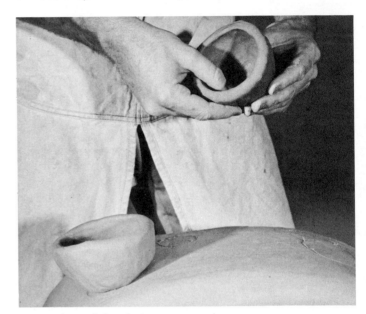

6. Weld solidly, then reinforce with clay coil.

7. Mark pinch-bowl placement on drum.

8. Score, add slip, and attach pinch bowls.

9. Paddle to insure solid joint.

leather-hard, then do any necessary smoothing with a damp sponge and modeling tool.

IRREGULAR SLAB FORMS

The large irregular form by Joe Hawley (pages 61, 62) combines slab and thrown forms in a most unusual and interesting manner. The body of such a piece may be quite varied in form and offers a great deal of opportunity for creative imagination.

In making this irregular form, a ⅜" thick rectangular slab was rolled out on a piece of cheesecloth, and the edges were immediately scored and coated with thick slip. Then a paper bag filled with excelsior was placed on half the single slab, and the other half was folded over so that the edges matched. (The bag and excelsior burn out on firing.) As the edges were solidly pinched together, the body contour was formed. The cheesecloth was then folded over the form to provide a supporting sling, and the cloth was suspended by clamping the top edges between two boards in a vise.

The cylindrical base and conical neck were then thrown, and all parts were permitted to become leather-hard. The form was then removed from the sling, and the joining parts of the base and neck were cut and pressed to the contour of the form. The joining surfaces were scored, coated with slip, placed in position, and worked vigorously together. A wooden weeding tool with metal prongs removed was used as a paddle for the curved

Irregular slab forms show variety, imagination. Joe Hawley

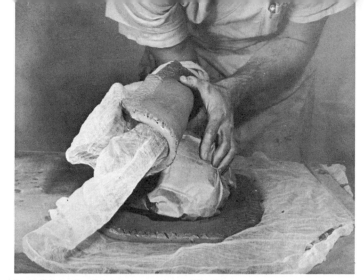

1. *Fold single slab over excelsior-filled bag.*

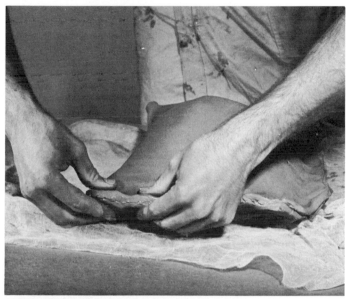

2. *Pinch scored and slip-coated edges solidly.*

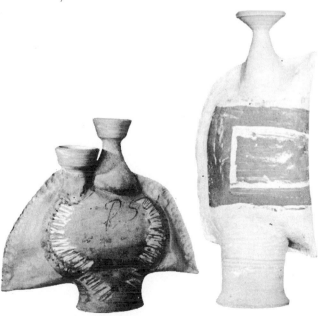

3. *Cheesecloth provides sling for support.*

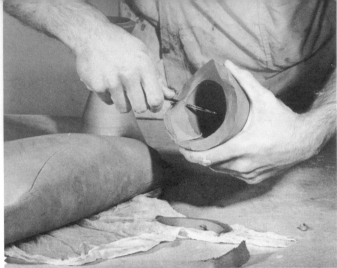

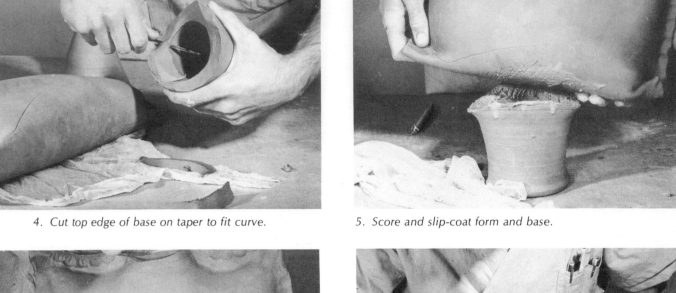

4. Cut top edge of base on taper to fit curve.

5. Score and slip-coat form and base.

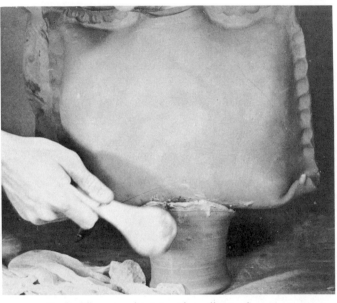

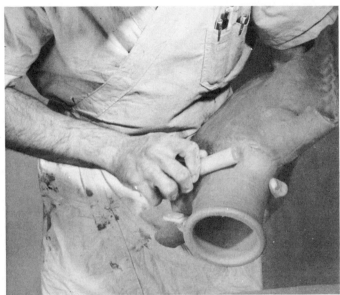

6. Paddle curved joint with mallet tool.

7. Weld joint with fettling knife handle.

8. Tapered joints fit over outside of form.

9. Paddle tapered, scored, slip-coated neck joint.

surfaces, and the handle of a fettling knife was used as a modeling tool where strong pressure was necessary. Joining edges of the foot and neck were tapered to fit over the outside of the form before being attached.

MOLDED SLABS

Matching sets of bowls for serving popcorn, soup, salad, and other foods are easily made by molding soft slabs in or over clay forms. When the form used is hollow and the clay slab is smoothed and pushed into it, it is known as a "press mold." The inside of the mold forms the outside of the pottery piece. Another type of mold used with slabs is the "drape mold." This is a convex shape and the slab is draped and smoothed over it to form the piece. In this case the outside of the mold forms the inside of the pot. Drape-molded forms will be most successful if pieces are made rather shallow.

MAKING A PRESS MOLD

Build this type of mold with thick rolls unless it is to be quite small—small forms can be shaped by pinching. The main requirement of the press mold is that it be free of bumps and irregularities on the inner surface. A foot can be carved directly in the mold bottom if desired. Foot curves should be gradual and easy, without sharp angles or corners which would not allow clay to move as it dries and shrinks. Foot rims can also be added to the outside of the press-molded form after it is leather-hard.

When the coiled or pinched clay form is completely dry, fire it to a dull red heat to make it durable for use.

MAKING A DRAPE MOLD

Making the drape or "hump" mold, as it is sometimes called, is actually a problem in modeling. Model a mound of clay to the desired form. Smooth by sponging the outer mold surface. The underside of the form may be hollowed to a mushroom-like form if desired, although this is not necessary. Do any hollowing after the clay is leather-hard. When the mold is completely dry, fire to a dull red heat.

USING MOLDS

You can use any clay for drape and press molding. Since clay must be shaped over or in the mold

PRESS MOLD. 1. Place slab in mold.

2. Pat into place, trim excess.

3. Smooth inside surface with sponge.

DRAME MOLD. 1. Place mold on top of slab.

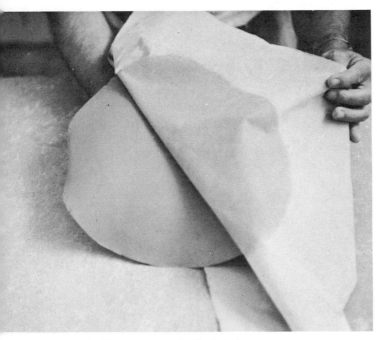

2. Turn over, peel off oilcloth.

3. Trim excess, smooth surface with sponge.

while still plastic, roll out slabs on a piece of cloth or canvas which you can lift with the slab on it. Invert cloth and clay over the form and lower it. Peel away cloth, and press clay into position either in or on the mold, starting at the mold center. The prime objective in molding is to achieve a bowl wall that is uniformly thick throughout; variations in thickness may cause the piece to warp or crack.

In smoothing walls, first use the wooden modeling tool to scrape away bumps and uneven spots, then use a dampened sponge to smooth them. Remove excess clay from around rims with a knife and smooth with a sponge. As soon as the clay is leather-hard and has begun to pull away from the mold, it can be removed from mold.

To remove a piece from a press mold, place a plaster bat on top of mold and invert it. Lift the mold, then sponge and round the pot rim. Add a foot made of a strip or coil if one is desired and has not been formed by the inside of the mold.

If the drape-molded shape is to have a foot, add it while the form is still supported by the mold. When all parts of the piece are leather-hard, lift it from the mold to finish drying.

BOX MOLDS

Large, straight-sided pots, planters, or lamp bases can be more easily made of clay slabs if these are supported by a box-like arrangement of boards. Make a four-sided box with open ends and inside dimensions equal to the outside dimensions required for the piece. If two corners of the box mold are solidly fastened and the other two joined by lapping and nailing—nails driven in only part way—the form can be easily removed by simply pulling the nails on the two lapped corners.

Form the large straight-sided pieces by pressing slabs inside the mold, which has been set on a plaster bat large enough to accommodate the entire mold. Round and strengthen joints at inside angles with fillets made of clay coils. Trim the rim level with the top edge of the mold.

If the piece is to be a plant container, cut a small drainage hole in the bottom. If it is to be a lamp base, make a small hole in the side near the bottom for the cord and add a top slab with any necessary openings for lamp fittings cut in it.

As soon as the clay stiffens and shrinks enough to pull away from the wooden form, remove the form. Use a wet sponge to round corners and edges, then set the piece aside on supporting bat until it is completely dry. Large pieces should dry slowly and should be covered with a damp cloth for 24 hours at the start of the drying period.

SLAB SCULPTURE

You'll find making small sculptures by this method both entertaining and easy. Results can be amusing and decorative, too. The method is a simple one—the slab is cut to a pattern and the figure is rounded and draped over a temporary support. As a beginning, you may want to use the pattern for the polar bear given here. You can, of course, develop your own patterns to make original figures.

To make the bear, first cut out a pattern from a folded sheet of paper. Lay it on a slab about ¼" thick which has been rolled on cloth that can be lifted. Prepare a support by making a tapered wad of clay about 3" high or use a small glass jar laid on its side in a wad of clay to keep it from rolling. Cover either type of support with paper toweling so that the slab will not stick to it.

Cut the clay around the pattern with the knife. Remove excess clay and allow the form to stiffen slightly. Then place a plaster bat on top of the clay and turn the bat, clay, and cloth over as one. Lift off bat and peel cloth from clay. Use both hands to lift and drape the clay over the prepared support. Bend sides, feet, and head to shape them. If the neck shows a tendency to droop, support it with a temporary clay post.

When the bear is leather-hard, add ears made of small triangles, joining them to the head with slip. Press in place and smooth joints with a modeling tool.

When the bear can stand alone, remove it from the support, and sponge and round all edges. Animals in sitting positions, or those with humped or curved backs, are better depicted as slab sculptures when they are made with patterns and slabs cut in two pieces. The engaging little squirrel shown here is an example of this type of form.

To make the squirrel according to the pattern given here, start with about 3½ pounds of

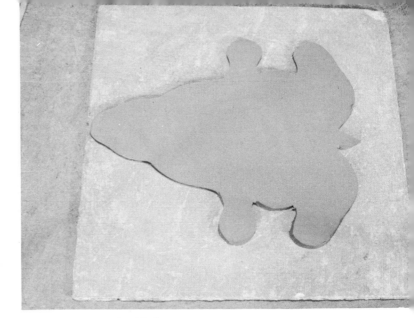

1. Cut bear from doubled paper pattern.

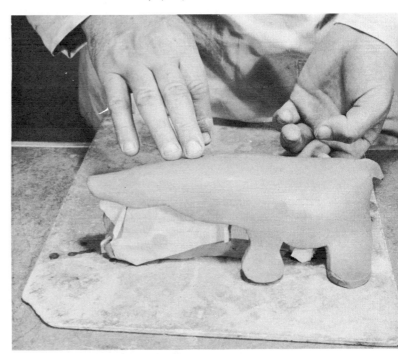

2. Form figure by draping around tapered clay wad.

3. Finished product glazed in cream, appropriate for polar bear. Triangular ears attached with slips.

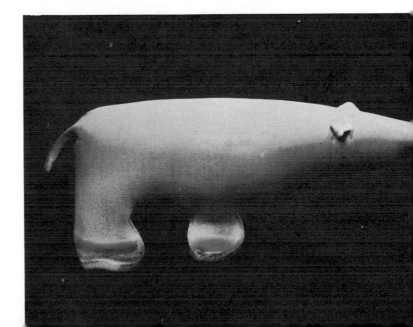

1. Duplicate halves cut from paper pattern.

medium-stiff wedged clay. Roll out a slab and cut out two matching squirrel shapes. While these stiffen to allow handling, prepare a tapered clay plug 4" high, with diameters of 1½" at the bottom and ¾" at top.

When the clay shapes can be lifted safely, assemble by placing one on either side of the upright plug. Pinch the edges of the two slabs together from the nose to the ears. Do not pinch the ears together—bend them outward instead. Pinch the edges of the body along the neck and the line next to tail. Pinch the top edges of the tail together and let the figure set for about an hour. Then shape tail, head, legs, and body. When the squirrel is leather-hard, remove the plug and seal all inside joints with a modeling tool. Round the edges with damp sponge and set the piece away to dry.

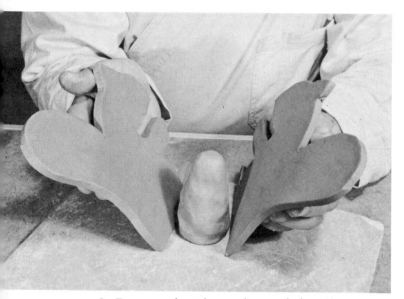

2. Two parts shaped around tapered plug.

3. Completed squirrel formed by pinching edges of two slabs together, allowing clay to set, then shaping tail, head, body.

Cut out doubled paper pattern.

Cut two matching shapes.

Mixed media sculpture entitled "Dancers" violates the principle of compactness. However the charming qualities introduced by the free use of fragile coils combined with slabs formed around crumpled newspaper more than compensate for the fragility of the piece. Vent holes were drilled into the bottom of the closed slab figures when they were leather-hard. Daisy Mah

7
Ceramic Sculpture

This phase of working with clay is the most fascinating of all to many potters. In this chapter we will consider methods and means of making large sculptures.

Clay for sculpture usually contains a fairly high proportion of reasonably coarse grog. Inclusion of grog does several things. First, it adds texture, which is often desirable when the piece is large and the clay is not to be covered with glaze. (Sculpture made from red or brown clays is often left unglazed.) Also, clay color can sometimes be made more interesting by using grog in a color that contrasts with that of the clay body. If the surface of the sculpture is to be smooth but not glazed, it can be sponged lightly with an elephant-ear sponge when nearly dry to bring out the grog color; emery cloth or sandpaper may be used to smooth the surface after firing. The addition of grog also opens the clay structure to make it more porous, which helps in drying and firing and also enables it to take up water readily if the work must be moistened during modeling.

Exact amounts of grog to add will depend on the effects desired and can be determined only by individual experiment. Up to 25 percent may be added, however, without destroying plastic quality of clay needed for sculptural purposes.

Clay sculptures will be best if expressed in compact forms fittingly designed for the material. It has been said that any sculpture should be formed so it can roll downhill—extended limbs or appendages would break off with such treatment—and while it is hardly advisable to treat any ceramic piece this way, it is suggested that you plan to keep your sculpture features tucked in rather than extended.

The most commonly used method in modeling sculpture is that of building up the main masses with small wads of clay. The whole figure is solidly built and roughly modeled to shape over the entire form. Refining of details is done when the clay has stiffened slightly. When solid pieces of any size are leather-hard they should be cut in half and halves should be hollowed until the walls are fairly uniform in thickness. The edges of the hollowed halves are then moistened, covered with slip, and rejoined. If openings do not comprise a part of the design, drill or pierce one or two small holes in the bottom to serve as air vents, which will be needed when the piece is fired. Pieces which set flat on the table may be hollowed from the bottom and need not be cut in half.

Quite small figures (those 3″ to 4″ in diameter), or those slightly larger which have had careful building and complete, slow drying, are often successfully fired without being hollowed. If much solid modeling is to be done, it is advisable to do the drying in a pottery drier (a closed cabinet with a means of maintaining a constant temperature of from 150 to 170 degrees F.).

The giraffe pictured is an example of modeling done solidly and subsequently hollowed. The body and neck were modeled from a mass of coarse, grogged clay. The legs and head were added as coils while the body rested in a clay cradle pedestal. The mane, ears, horns, and tail were added when the form was leather-hard. After modeling was completed, the piece was

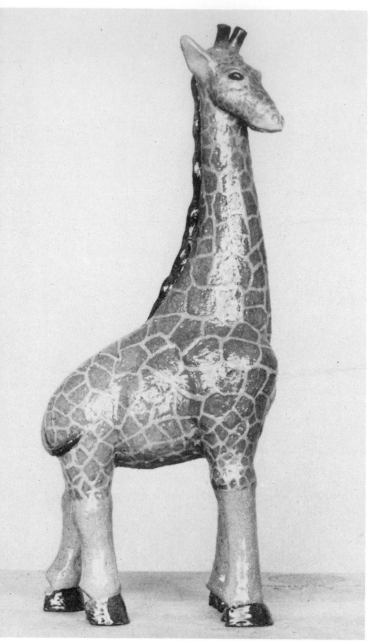

Stoneware giraffe, 20" high, built solid and then when leather-hard cut in two, hollowed out, and reassembled.

painted with light and dark slips. The finished animal, which is 20" high, was glazed with transparent glaze and fired to cone 4.

Coil-built figures are built hollow. The main masses of the figure are made as coiled shapes, with each coil welded inside and out as the building progresses. Refinements and additions to the form are made when the clay has stiffened but is not yet leather-hard.

There is, of course, a tremendous variety in what can be done with coil-built sculpture. Animals, human figures, abstract decorative figures, and utilitarian objects of various sizes can be made. The figures can be glazed or left unglazed.

The coil-built lantern and elephant illustrated nearby will give you an idea of two of the many possibilities.

COIL-BUILT LANTERN

To build the bird-cage type of lantern shown, roll out several long lengths of coil about ⅝" in diameter. Drape vertical coils over a sheet metal form, or use a clay hump covered with paper towel. Next, attach horizontal coils to the vertical ones, using slip. When leather-hard, carefully remove cage from form and mount on a leather-hard slab. Reinforce with coil on top of slab. Add a looped-coil handle.

PINCH SCULPTURE

Interesting and decorative sculpture can be made by the pinch process. The animal on the next page, by John Leary, is particularly appealing. To make it, pinch a bowl whose rim is thicker than the rest of its wall. When the bowl is of the desired size, squeeze it so that the edges of the rim come together, but do not flatten the form. Weld the edges and smooth the joint. Do any necessary shaping and set the piece aside to become leather-hard. Make legs, score, and attach them to the form with slip. Press the legs firmly into position, weld joints, and do any final shaping. Paddle lightly for subtlety of form. Incise eyes and decoration, paint, and use drybrush techniques to add colored slip over the back.

SLAB SCULPTURE

A decorative household guardian made by John Leary (page 73) doubles as a candle sconce. The highly abstract figure with a small, double-pinched bowl head has a face in back as well as in front,

(Above) Coil-built earthenware elephant, 3' long × 20" high, has a vent hole that was punched in the stomach when the piece was leather-hard. After being biscuit-fired, the elephant was glazed with a gray-green matt glaze.

Coil-built lantern stands on flat surface or can be hung by chain. John Leary

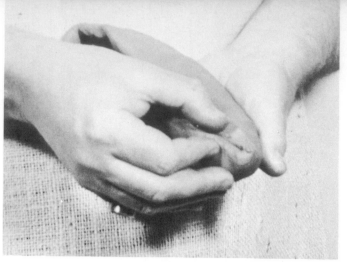

PINCH SCULPTURE. 1. Squeeze edges of rim.

2. Weld the joint, holding form carefully.

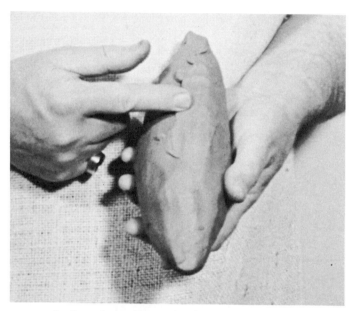

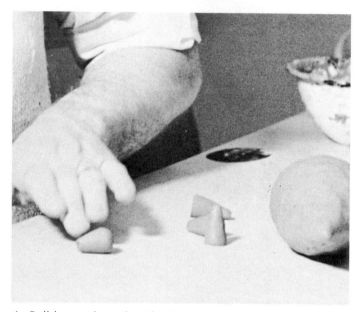

3. Smooth the joint, using fingers.

4. Roll legs and attach with slip.

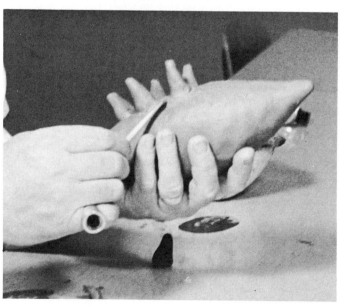

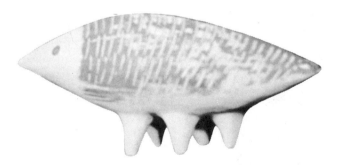

Eyes and decoration are incised, and colored slip is brushed over back. John Leary

5. Weld legs to leather-hard body.

This complex slab sculpture was formed around crumpled newspaper. The piece shows masterful use of porcelain. It was glazed and fired at cone 9. Carol Barry

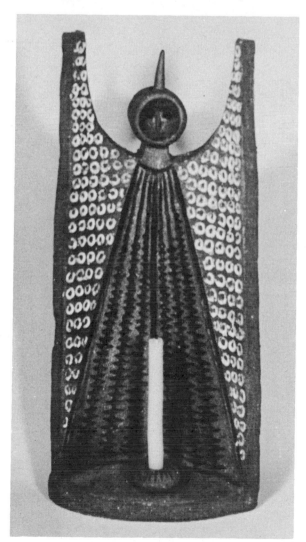

Candle holder waxed when leather hard, scratched, painted with colored slips, biscuit-fired high. John Leary

thus watches both back and front doors at the same time.

To make a piece like it, roll a rectangular slab to ½" thickness and cut to the desired size. Lightly sketch an arc at one end of the rectangle, using the point of a fettling knife or a lead pencil. Cut through the slab and remove the arc. Use the arc as a base for the figure. Drape oilcloth and then the slab over a cylindrical form—a rolling pin or a glass jar will do. When the slab is leather-hard, score joints, coat with slip, and assemble as for other slab pieces. Attach a pinched candle holder and double-pinched head. Coat the form with wax, incise a design through the wax, and paint over the incising with different colored slips. This sculpture is left unglazed.

THROWN PADDLED FIGURE

The variations possible in thrown sculpture are virtually unlimited. In Chapter 9, you will see how

THROWN PADDLED FIGURE. 1. Detail with paddle handle.

THROWN MODELED FIGURE. 1. Arm outline cut through.

2. Side of paddle develops head features.

2. Arm brought forward and body pressed together.

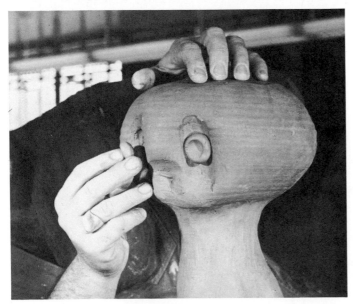

3. Balls of clay for eyes attached with slip.

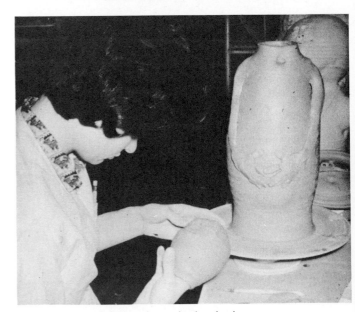

3. Head is modeled and attached to body.

wheel sculpture can retain the quality of thrown forms. The illustrations in the left column on page 74 show how Claude Horan retains qualities that are characteristic of wheel-built pieces in a thrown and paddled sculpture.

THROWN MODELED FIGURE

Maryann Gravitt does not paddle her sculpture but models from both inside and outside, accenting modeled areas by cutting through the wall and by adding portions of the figure as slabs. The second series of photographs on page 74 explains this process.

MODELING TOOLS

As always, fingers are the first tools in clay modeling techniques. There are several tools you may want to add to your equipment. Modeling tools are available with wire and metal loops of various shapes at ends of their wooden handles. Knives and wooden modeling tools in numerous shapes and sizes are also available. Choose from these according to your needs, but try to use the largest tool compatible with the work to avoid small and niggling effects.

GENERAL SUGGESTIONS

The principles of making clay sculpture are much the same as those of making such forms in any other sculptural medium. Although the esthetics of the matter are outside the scope of this book, the following suggestions should be of help in handling clay to make sculptured forms:

Start the figure on a base large enough to hold it, and place it so that you can turn the work continually. Work around the entire figure, developing detail at about the same rate all over it rather than concentrating on a detail which might later prove to be misplaced. Turning and working around the piece will enable you to see it as a three-dimensional object.

Add moist clay to moist clay surfaces to build and fasten clay parts. If some part of the figure proves to be over-built, take a little more fresh clay than is needed, bring it to an under-built

Thrown and paddled stoneware sculpture. Claude Horan

stage, and then use it to replace the formed clay until the amount is right. Bear in mind that building is adding clay—not pushing, pulling, or rubbing it from one place to another. The finished shape should look as if it has been made of clay.

If the figure is to be glazed (large ones are often left unglazed), this should be taken into account in the designing. Dull, matte glazes are usually preferred, because the non-reflecting surfaces allow planes to be seen without the visual confusion often present when highly reflecting, shiny glazes are used. Small figures are occasionally accented with sections of enamel-like opaque glaze on a background of unglazed clay body color, or wholly covered for various decorative effects.

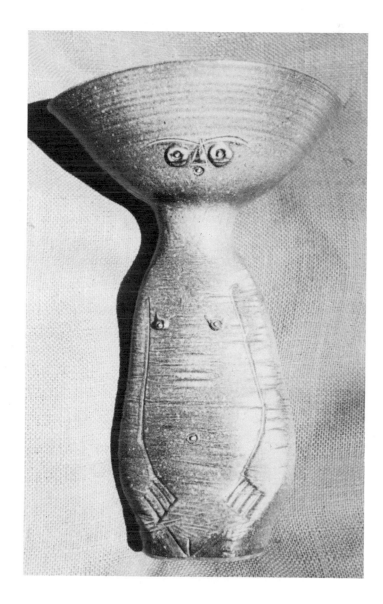

Thrown sculpture that was first trimmed then inverted and paddled. When the piece was leather-hard, the pattern was impressed and black and white slips were painted onto the desired areas. Then the face was sgraffitoed through the white slip. Fred Lucero

8
Decorative Processes

Surface decoration can be added to the pottery form in many ways. Decoration of the form may be thought of first, perhaps, as a coating of glaze, appropriate in color and kind to fit both the shape of the piece and its ultimate use. Glazes in many colors are also used to paint designs or patterns chosen to produce certain textures and effects, as well as for other forms of embellishment. Since glazing is one of the primary ways of decorating pottery, an entire section of this chapter is devoted to the process. There are, however, a number of other ways of adding decorations to the surfaces of your wares, which you may also want to consider.

The matter of adding surface decoration to a pottery form must be decided upon according to individual preference. You are the potter—the choice is yours. As skills develop, you will find a tendency to think of pottery forms as finished realities—complete with planned decorative effects. In the meantime, you can experiment with a few basic decorating processes. (A number of these will be described in this chapter.) Use tiles or clay slabs as "sketch pads"; these can be fired, glazed, and filed away for ready reference. You might, for instance, make several 4" or 6" tiles and make samplers of the various processes to be described. After biscuit-firing your samplers, apply various glazes in parallel stripes across each tile and then glost-fire them so that you can see both the glaze colors and how they appear when used with particular techniques.

IMPRESSED DECORATION

Almost any familiar object can be used to impress texture or pattern in damp clay surfaces. Use the end of your wooden modeling tool, a pebble, the edge of an apricot pit or a piece of coarsely woven cloth. You can, if you like, design decorative motifs and carve them in wood, plaster, clay, or linoleum to make clay stamps. One such stamp might be designed as your personal trademark.

Impressed decoration can be added to your clay tile or slab as soon as it is hard enough to be picked up and turned over without losing shape. If it becomes too hard, it will crack or break when impressions are made. Tile can be brought back into condition for impressing by being covered with a damp cloth for a few minutes. If impressed decorations are made on the outside of a pot, support the wall on the inside at the point of impression with your left hand.

CARVED DECORATIONS

Carved decorations may consist of incised or excised lines or areas, pierced areas made by removing clay completely, or a combination of all three forms of carving.

Incised decoration is made by carving the motif or pattern into the surface. Such carving lowers the pattern, leaving the background areas as thick as the original clay. The pattern may be linear or mass or a combination of line and mass. Any blunt

Excised decoration is done when clay is leather-hard.

point, such as that of a lead pencil or a "bobby" pin fastened to a stick, will make an incising tool for linear patterns. Large areas can be cut or scraped away with the loop end of the wire modeling tool or the end of the knife blade. This technique should be practiced upon a medium-stiff, leather-hard tile.

In excised decoration, the background is lowered or carved out of the clay surface to leave the elements forming the design motif at the original level. The lowered background may be left smooth or various textures may be impressed or incised into it. Tools used are the same as those used for incising, and a medium-stiff tile should be used as a sampler.

Pierced carving calls for the removal of the areas that form either the motif or the background. Clay for this type of carving must not be too stiff or it will crack and break during the process.

DECORATING WITH SLIP

Decorating slips are clays mixed with sufficient water to make them the consistency of thick cream. You can buy slips in many colors from your ceramic supply dealer, or if the clay you are using fires white, cream, or buff, you can add metallic oxides or stains according to the table given at the end of this chapter to make your own slips. Color ingredients should be thoroughly ground into the slip with a mortar and pestle and rubbed through an 80-mesh screen for use in decorating. Mortars and mesh screens are available at ceramic supply stores.

SLIP PAINTING

Slip may be applied with a brush on unfired, leather-hard pieces. Textural variations are achieved by using slip in thick or thin dilutions, by light or heavy application, and using a dry-brush technique. Brush painting with slip on thirsty dried clay calls for a different technique than other forms of brush painting. The dry clay rapidly draws moisture from the liquid slip, and the slip is actually laid in place with the brush rather than drawn along with it as in enameling, for instance.

SLIP TRACING

This decorative process has been used on pottery made by the Romans, the English, the Pennsylvania Dutch settlers in our own country, and by European potters. The slip tracing cup was made

Stoneware planter with incising used as texture. When the piece was leather-hard, the wall was cut through and pressed outward at the incisions. Slabs attached inside reinforce the cut areas and seal the planter against leakage. The piece was thrown with an attached saucer to catch water from the drainage holes near the bottom of the wall. Denise Vogel

Detail of a large, flat stoneware bowl. The design represents an Andean woman and child and was applied in gray, red, brown, and black slips done in sgraffito. Marguerite Wildenhain

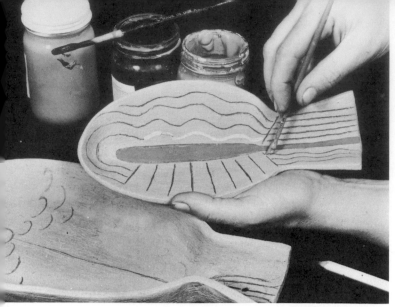

Slip is laid in place with brush, not drawn along clay. Clay should be leather-hard.

of clay shaped to fit the hand, with quills or tubes protruding from one side of the cup. As the cup was held in the hand for use, the tubes stuck out between the fingers and the open top of the cup was covered by the palm of the hand. When the palm was slightly lifted, the slip would flow through the tubes; when lowered, the palm acted as a lid and stopped the flow of slip. You can, if you wish, make such a multiple-tubed cup. A rubber syringe, the type used for ears or infant hygiene, will make a satisfactory substitute. Fill the syringe with thick slip so that no air is held in the bulb to cause the slip to splash or splatter. Uniform and even pressure on the bulb as the tube is drawn along the lines of the motif should result in an even flow of slip. Do slip tracing on leather-hard clay.

SGRAFFITO

This is an Italian word meaning "scratched through" and the sgraffito form of pottery decoration is done by scratching a pattern through a slip coat to reveal the color of the clay body underneath. Apply the coat of slip to leather-hard clay by brushing, dipping, or spraying. Let the slip dry until it no longer sticks to your fingers in handling, then scratch lines with the blunt point of a lead pencil or a bobby pin, and scrape the areas with a wire-ended modeling tool or a knife point.

MISHIMA

This form of decoration was developed by the Koreans and named by the Japanese. Decorations on the first pieces embellished in this manner, which were imported into Japan, resembled the writing on the Japanese Almanac. Consequently, the name of this form of decoration means "Almanac writing."

Mishima decoration is made by first impressing, incising, or excising the motif into the clay surface and then covering it with a thin coating of slip in a color that contrasts with the clay body. When the slip is no longer sticky, sponge or scrape it from the raised portions of the design. A thin film of slip left on some of the raised areas serves to add interest to the textural quality. Try this on a portion of the excised, incised, or impressed tile decorations.

Eye-dropper or small syringe can be used to apply slip in lines, dots.

Colored slip can be incised to show clay color beneath: process called "sgraffito." Doris Aller

Stoneware vase, 12" high, showing children with kites carved in red, blue, brown, and black slips. Marguerite Wildenhain

(Left) Stoneware vase, 14" high, entitled "Beach Party" illustrates sgraffito done through slip decoration. Marguerite Wildenhain

(Above) Decorative stoneware bowl done in four underglaze colors on a light background, coated with a transparent crackle glaze, and fired to cone 4.

Thrown and slab-constructed sculpture displays a combination of matt glaze and deerskin leather epoxied onto the modeled section of the form. Michael O'Donnell

Apply white matt, partial quick dip in dark gloss for pleasing contrast.

STAMPED OR STIPPLED SLIP

Still another way to use slip is to stipple it on leather-hard ware with a sponge. Add water to make a thinner than customary slip for this. Thin slip can also be used with rubber stamps on leather-hard or dry clay.

MODELED DECORATION

Clay shapes can be modeled and fastened to a tile or pot surface when the clay can be handled. Use the wooden modeling tool to round the edges of the applied motifs and press them into place. Dry pieces with such decorations very slowly, checking periodically to see that the applied shapes do not loosen.

UNDERGLAZE DECORATION

Underglaze painting is the process in which a biscuited piece is first painted with a special coloring substance and then glazed with a transparent glaze and fired to the appropriate temperature for the glaze and ware. Almost any clay can be used, but white, cream, or buff bodies produce the best effects.

Commercially prepared colors can be easily obtained from a ceramic supply dealer. These are made by calcining together various metallic oxides and other ceramic materials. They usually come in powdered form and must be mixed with a medium such as glycerine before being brushed on the piece.

GLAZING

Ceramic glazes are complex fusions which have been classified as both solid solutions and super-cooled liquids. The beginner or hobbyist will better understand glazes and glazing if he thinks of glazes simply as a coating of glass which has fused to the surface of the clay during the firing process.

Although one function of a glaze is to enhance the piece, it also seals the clay surface to make it more easily cleaned and sanitary in use. This is most important in tableware and of little or no importance in other kinds of ware. Therefore, the first consideration in selecting a glaze for a particular piece can be either function or appearance.

Again, decorating your pottery by applying glaze is a matter of personal choice. There are

Stoneware vase illustrating a crackle glaze pattern of excellent uniformity. James Lovera

Covered stoneware jar shows one glaze poured over another to create interesting color and texture variations. Philip Nakamura

Wax emulsion painted on dark body, white matt brushed over for glazed and unglazed areas. Claude Horan

many kinds of glaze to choose from. Glazes may be colorless, adding a sealing coat over the clay body but not concealing it; they may be colored and transparent, opalescent, semi-transparent, or opaque. Most glazes are glossy and highly reflecting. Some have matte or semi-matte surfaces, which are dull or partially dulled and non-reflecting.

In selecting a glaze, bear in mind that a brightly colored, highly glossy glaze can be appropriately used on a small bowl or vase to impart a jewel-like elegance to it. But the same glaze might prove inappropriate for a larger form, making it only gaudy or vulgar. On such a form, a matte glaze would perhaps be a better choice. On the other hand, dull coatings are thick and rather heavy; while they look good on massive pieces, they can overwhelm a smaller piece and may completely obliterate any small detail.

PURCHASING PREPARED GLAZES

Glazes are composed of powdered chemicals and minerals which assume the positions of bases, acids, and neutrals in the total composition. Differences in color result from the addition of color-producing metallic oxides, either raw or as prepared stains. The study of glaze composition is one of the most fascinating in the whole pottery field. As a budding potter, you will take advantage of the prepared glazes and glaze powders which you can purchase. Some simple experiments in making glazes are given later in this chapter in the hope that you will eventually develop your own.

Even in the relatively simple matter of purchasing prepared glazes there are several things to consider. Glazes are usually classified according to color, type (glossy or matte, transparent or opaque, etc.), and maturing temperature, which is designated by cone number. (See Chapter 11 for an explanation of cone-temperature relationship.) The glaze maturing temperature should be the same as that of the clay it is to be used on. Potters say that glaze must "fit" the body—one that does not fit will show defects in the form of crazing or shivering. Ceramic dealers sell clays and glazes compounded to be successfully used together. Ask your dealer if the clay you are using should be glazed with the glazes you intend to buy.

Also, buy only those glazes that will mature at temperatures that are possible in the kiln in which your glazed wares will be fired.

MIXING AND APPLYING GLAZE

If you have purchased powdered glazes, you must first mix these with a sufficient amount of water to make a mixture about as thick as whipping cream. Glazes sold in jars containing the proper amount of water need only be well stirred.

Glaze can be applied to ware in several ways. The common methods are brushing, pouring, dipping, and spraying. A soft varnish brush about 1″ wide is needed for brushing glaze. Interiors of such pieces as bowls are often glazed by putting glaze in the piece, turning and rolling it until the inside is covered, then pouring off any excess glaze. The outside can be glazed by pouring as well. Place the piece on a screen or sticks placed across the top of a pan and pour glaze over it.

Dipping requires a larger amount of glaze than pouring or brushing—enough to allow complete immersion of the piece—and a vessel large enough to hold the glaze. The piece is merely submerged in the glaze for a few seconds, then removed.

Glaze is usually thinned for spraying. This can be done in a household spray such as those used for insecticides, etc., but an electric gun and compressor made for glaze spraying will do an easier and better job. Place the piece to be sprayed on a bench whirler, turning it so that all parts of the piece receive an equal amount of glaze.

All of these methods have advantages and disadvantages. Pouring and brushing require the least equipment and will therefore serve the beginner the best. You should apply glaze to only those pieces which have been biscuit-fired. Commercial potteries often glaze greenware and bring both clay and glaze to maturity in a single fire, but such a practice is highly inadvisable for schools, studios, or the beginner working at home.

To glaze a biscuit-fired piece with brushing or pouring methods, first thoroughly sponge it with a clean wet sponge to remove dust and to partially fill the pores of the clay with water. This sponging will reduce the tendency of the brush and glaze to stick to the piece and overload the surface in spots.

Glaze both sides of flat bowls or plates and outside walls of upright forms by brushing glaze on with short, patting strokes. Some unevenness is inevitable, but since melting and flowing of the glaze will level it to some degree, it is not particularly harmful. You will need to apply two, or possibly three, coats before reaching a total thickness of approximately ¹/₁₆″. Cover the inside of the piece first, either by brushing or pouring. Pour glaze into the form, then tip it over a pan and swirl and revolve it as you pour glaze out. Do this quickly or the damp wall may take up an overly thick coat, which may crack before firing or crawl during firing. A coat that is too thick may also run down the sides of the piece to form a pool in the bottom, which might possibly break the piece as it cools after firing.

Since glaze does run when fired (some more than others, due to composition), give the rim edges an extra coat. When the glaze has dried so that it is no longer sticky, scrape and sponge the glaze from the bottom surface of the foot and remove about ¹/₁₆″ of it from the outside bottom edge of the wall. These precautions should be taken to prevent the glaze from running down and sticking to the kiln shelf.

When the glazed piece has dried thoroughly it will be ready for glost-firing.

PARTIAL GLAZE

When a colored body is used, interesting decorative effects may result from glazed and unglazed areas on the same piece. Regardless of the treatment of the outside, the inside surface should be completely glazed if the piece is to be used as a container. To have glazed and unglazed areas on a piece, use wax emulsion from a ceramic supply house or make your own from 1 part paraffin and 1 part kerosene heated over a hot plate until the paraffin has melted. Then paint the areas with the mixture where you want no glaze. Be sure the glaze is not too thick. Apply it by brushing, pouring, dipping, or spraying after the waxed areas have dried. The wax will resist the glaze coat; when fired, the piece will have a contrasting texture of glazed and unglazed areas.

POURING GLAZE

The decorative effects created by pouring glaze are many and varied. Some glazes are more suitable for pouring than others, owing to their compositions. However, most glazes can be used satisfactorily after a little practice. To glaze a pot by pouring, place two 1″ square, well-sanded hardwood boards across a large pan. Wax the foot of the piece and about ½″ of wall above foot, then sponge the piece with a clean damp sponge. Glaze the piece inside, then invert it on the boards over the center of the pan and use an enameled metal pitcher to pour the glaze over the outside surface of the piece. Move the pitcher around as you pour.

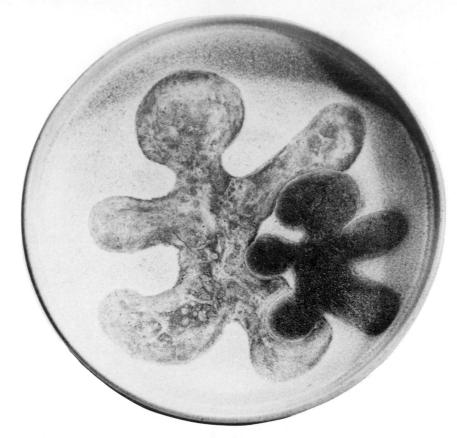

Stoneware bowl with light green matt glaze background was inlaid with a brown and darker green glaze of the same basic composition.

On this piece, a single color (black) was superimposed on RLM majolica glaze and fired to cone 3. The texture in the trunk seems to have formed because the black was painted in both heavy and diluted solutions. The black glaze hand-ground with a mortar and pestle.

As soon as the glaze surface no longer glistens, pour a second coat if desired. As soon as the glazed piece is dry enough so that it does not stick to your fingers, pour a glaze of a contrasting color over the surface in the desired pattern.

DIPPING

To dip-glaze a pot with a smooth, uniform coating requires enough glaze and a large enough container to completely submerge the piece in a single dipping; only small pieces should be dip-glazed. Wax the foot and about ½" up the wall from the foot, and permit the wax to dry. For small-necked forms, pour the glaze inside the piece, sponge the outside with a damp sponge, and cover the top with a flat, circular piece of rigid sheet metal the same size or slightly larger than the outside diameter of the top rim of the pot. Hold the metal disc in place with the thumb, support the foot rim with your fingers, and submerge the piece in the glaze. Then set it aside and touch up any bare spots on the rim with a finger dipped into the glaze.

Open forms are usually dipped without using metal disc on the rims; both the inside and outside are glazed at the same time. A quick dip of part of the form in a different colored glaze should be done while the first coat is still damp. A wax pattern may be painted on the first glaze coat and the piece may then be completely or partly dipped in a glaze of a different color before the first coat dries. If the first coat dries completely before the second coat is added, the second glaze may crack and peel off or crawl when fired.

CRACKLE GLAZE

A crackle glaze may be desired for its decorative effect on certain pieces. Crackle is commonly considered to be controlled crazing, which means that it is intentional, not an accident, and results in a crackle pattern the potter feels is attractive on the piece. Crazing is caused by unequal thermal expansion and contraction between the body and the glaze. For most potters, developing a glaze that will not craze is difficult enough to make them use crackle glazes sparingly. But there are pieces on which a crackle glaze can be a very desirable decorative feature. However, remember that crackle glazes should not be used on containers for liquids unless the clay body is sufficiently vitrified to prevent sweating, which can ruin varnished surfaces.

Assuming we have a glaze which does not craze and we want to make it into a crackle glaze, there are some simple procedures we might follow. First, we can use a clay body which will be under-fired (soft and porous) at the temperature at which the glaze matures. Second, if we are mixing our own glaze, we can leave out some of the clay that is part of the glaze composition. Third, we can add calcium phosphate (bone ash) to the glaze. Any of these procedures should cause the glaze to crackle during or soon after firing. You can rub India ink over the surface of a fired glaze to stain the crackle.

INLAID GLAZE PAINTING

Inlaid glaze painting is done on a biscuited piece. The piece is soaked in water for about 1½ minutes, rubbed dry, and covered with a ⅛" coating of glaze. When the glaze coat dries, the design is sketched on top of it in pencil. The outlines of the design are incised and the area inside is scraped away with a thin needle or knife point. The exposed area is then coated with a ⅛" layer of a different colored glaze.

SUPERIMPOSED GLAZE PAINTING

In this process, also called on-glaze and in-glaze decoration, the color decoration is laid on top of a coating of unfired glaze. The clay used for such a piece should be hard and durable, and the glaze should be one that will not run when molten, or it will distort the decoration.

The color decoration is usually made by mixing a portion of the glaze—in powdered form—with quantities of 5 to 20 percent metallic coloring oxides or earth pigments. The mixture is well ground on a ball mill, mixed with a medium such as glycerine or gum tragacanth solution, and blended together with a palette knife. When fired, the color decoration soaks into the glaze.

SOLUBLE SALTS DECORATION

In this form of decoration, the coloring agents are applied either under the glaze to the biscuited ware or on top of the unfired glaze. Commercially available colorants are saturated solutions of sulfates or nitrates of various metals; these are incorporated into the glaze and develop their colors during firing.

(Left) Shallow earthenware bowl decorated with metallic carbonate and a soluble salt solution. The piece was made of Fetzer red clay, bisquited to cone 06, then glazed with SF #7 glaze. The glaze was not coated with gum solution because maximum absorption was necessary to keep the soluble salt solution from spreading.

(Below) Siamese-twin pots were thrown, attached when leather-hard, bisquited, and only partly glazed by pouring. Judy Omai

(Right) Two covered stoneware jars showing the contrast between a very dry, matt ash glaze (left) and a glaze with a silky matt texture (right). John Leary

MIXING GLAZES. 1. *Weigh ingredients on scale.*

2. *Add water to glaze in mortar and pestle.*

3. *Apply glaze to test tiles and label tiles.*

GLAZE FAULTS AND DEFECTS

Crazing may prove to be an actual defect in a glaze. The hundreds of tiny cracks all over the surface of the glaze, which are characteristic of this fault, may appear during firing or as the piece cools. While crackled glazes are used for the effects mentioned earlier, unintended crackling can actually prove harmful to the piece.

Crazing may be the result of too thick an application of glaze, or of an imperfect fit of glaze to clay body.

Another common fault is known as crawling. In this case, the glaze gathers in bunches or raised sections and leaves other areas bare. This is commonly due to dust or grease on the biscuit ware, or to an overly generous application of glaze. To prevent crawling, avoid handling biscuit ware—oil from the hands can cause crawling. Sponge the piece to remove dust, and try to keep the coating of glaze about 1/16" thick.

Pinholes or small circular pits in the glaze are usually caused by gas bubbles that result when carbonaceous materials are burned from the glaze. This fault can be corrected by firing more slowly or to a higher temperature. Pinholing is also caused when sandpaper is used to smooth clay. Sandpaper is not a ceramic tool and sanding ceramic surfaces is not a desirable practice. It can be ruinous when the pieces are to be subsequently glazed, as the flints and various natural and synthetic minerals used to coat sandpaper are often incompatible with glaze ingredients—bits of these substances ground into a clay surface cause defects in the glaze.

Devitrification is recognized by a rough scum on the glaze surface. It is caused by too much silica in the glaze and can be corrected by an addition of china clay. A rough and sandy glaze may be the result of too thin a glaze application, insufficient firing, or a glaze ingredient that was not sufficiently ground.

Sulfuring may result from sulfur in the fuel used to fire the kiln, in the water, in a coloring oxide, or in other glaze ingredients. The result may be a blistered, dry, or shriveled glaze. Blisters are also sometimes the result of too short a firing period or the presence of smoke in the kiln. Check for cracks in the muffle if smoke is suspected; try distilled water or change the glaze ingredients if sulfur seems to be the cause of the trouble.

GLAZE-MAKING EXPERIMENTS

Here is a relatively simple method of experimenting with glaze compositions. It requires no knowledge of chemistry and only the most elementary knowledge of arithmetic. You will need a commercial glaze frit, an amount of bentonite, a balance scale which weighs in grams, a mixing bowl, a 60-mesh screen, a small mortar and pestle, three or four watercolor brushes, a 1" varnish brush, and a black ceramic marking pencil.

The first ingredient you will need is a commercial glaze frit. Frit is a carefully calculated and compounded glass which has been fused and powdered. Frits, identified by number, are sold at ceramic supply houses (see Suppliers List). Choose a frit with a maturing point within the firing range of the kiln available. There are many glaze frits, each with a different chemical composition. Any of the following will produce interesting results: #71—contains lead, sodium, alumina, and silica; #24—contains lead, sodium, potassium, calcium, alumina, boron, silica, and zirconium; #3304— contains lead, sodium, alumina, and silica; #3110 —contains potassium, sodium, calcium, magnesium, alumina, boron, and silica. Purchase an amount of one of these, as well as some bentonite.

Your balance scale should have a bar marked in 1/10 grams and be capable of weighing 10 grams. You should also have weights that include one or two 200-gram, one 100-gram, one 50-gram, two 20-, two 2-, and one each of 10-, 5- and 1-gram weights.

Make twenty-five or fifty test tiles by rolling out a clay slab ¼" thick and cutting it into strips 1¼" wide and 3" long. Bend the strips to form L's. Punch a ¼" hole at center of the upright part of the tile. Biscuit-fire the tiles at the temperature to be used for your ware.

Be sure the scale is balanced. When it is in balance, the needle between the pans will remain stationary at the center line. The weight on the bar must be at the extreme left. Place weights totaling 97 grams in the pan on the right. Place the frit on the left pan until the needle stops at the center line on the indicator. Place the weighed frit (97 grams) in a mixing bowl. Remove the weights from the pan and move the weight on the bar until the left edge is in line with the number 3 on the bar. Place powdered bentonite in the left pan until the needle

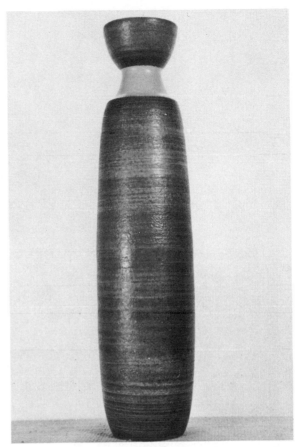

Tall, symmetrical bottle with brown and tan matt glaze.

Whimsical covered earthenware bowl was glazed in glossy black; hinged device for locking was finished in liquid gold. Michel Cole

again indicates a balance. Add the weighed bentonite to the frit and stir them together.

The bentonite and frit will form the basic glaze composition. Use the varnish brush to work the mixture through the screen twice; if there is a residue left in the screen, grind it in a mortar with pestle until it will pass through the mesh. Put these combined ingredients in a covered jar and identify it with a label stating the number of the frit used and that the mixture contains 97 percent frit plus 3 percent bentonite (a total of 100 percent).

To make a test of the base mixture for firing, weigh out 10 grams and place it in the mortar. Adding one drop of water at a time, grind the mixture with pestle until it has the consistency of medium-weight whipping cream. Brush this on the inside surfaces of a test tile. Use the black marking pencil to label the back of the tile to indicate the glaze composition as you did on the jar label. Fire the test tile.

ANALYZING TEST RESULTS

Examine the fired test tile and consider how it might be improved; what changes you would like to make in it. Additions of various glaze materials in weighed percentages will improve the glaze fit if crazing is present; make the glaze more, or less, fluid; vary the glaze texture; make it opaque; or add color to it. The effects of some of the materials commonly used to vary glazes are listed in the following paragraphs:

Additions of powdered white lead, red lead, litharge, borax, and soda ash in amounts of 5 to 15 percent will lower the melting point and increase fluidity.

The addition of rutile and titanium dioxide in amounts of 5 to 15 percent produce a matte texture and may make the glaze cream or buff colored.

Additions of ball clay, china clay, or kaolin in amounts of 5 to 25 percent will raise the melting point of the glaze, may help crazing, and in larger percentages will produce matte texture.

Additions of tin oxide, Zircopax, Ultrox, and other opacifying compounds may raise the fusion point of the glaze and help in correcting crazing. Usually 5 to 10 percent is sufficient to make the glaze opaque or white.

Additions of feldspar or whiting in amounts of 5 to 25 percent will increase viscosity, may help the glaze fit and raise the fusion point, and tend to develop a matte texture.

Flint increases viscosity, raises the fusion point, and may cause or correct crazing. Add in amounts of 10 to 20 percent.

For purposes of illustration, we will assume that the first test tile of the base glaze was satisfactory in gloss, but that the glaze was slightly too fluid and had crazed somewhat. Record these observations in a notebook set aside for this purpose. Give the test tile a number and transfer this number to the noted observations about the tile. Keep the tile also.

The next step in the glaze experiment is to correct the faults of crazing and over-fluidity in the base glaze. A study of the materials just listed and their effects will help you select one to improve the base glaze. In this case, we will add china clay to correct over-fluidity and crazing in this base glaze.

Throughout this series of experiments all materials will be added as plus percentages to the original 100 percent total of frit and bentonite. We now propose to add 5 percent to the original 100. To do this, weigh out 10 grams of the base mixture and place it in mortar. Weigh ½ gram of china clay. Remember that .1 gram (1/10 gram) equals 1 percent of ten grams and .5 gram (½ gram) equals 5 percent of 10 grams; we are adding 5 percent of china clay to our original mixture as a plus addition.

Grind the new mixture with water in mortar as before, apply it to the test tile, label the back of the tile and fire it. Make additional tests using 10, 15, 20, and 25 percent additions of china clay. Fire them and record the results.

We will assume that the glaze with the addition of 15 percent of china clay is no longer too fluid or crazed. If this series had not solved the problem, another material would have been added and the work would have been repeated.

Adjust the remaining basic mixture by adding 15 percent china clay to it. This is accomplished by first weighing the remainder; there should be 50 grams left. Add 7.5 grams china clay to this and screen the combined materials twice.

To make tests to produce an opaque glaze, weigh the adjusted base mixture into five equal parts of 11.5 grams each. To the first part add .2 gram tin oxide. To the second part add .4 gram; to the third, .6 gram; to the fourth, .8 gram, and to the fifth, 1 gram of tin oxide. Prepare the tiles, fire, make records and observations, and select the best.

To carry on with the sample experiment, we will assume that the 8 percent addition of tin oxide gave the most satisfactory results. This would make the glaze composition as follows: frit, 97 grams; bentonite, 3 grams; china clay, 15 grams; and tin, 8 grams. Mix several hundred grams of this glaze composition, screen it thoroughly, and you are ready to make experiments for color.

Using the metallic oxides listed in the table on page 98, run a complete series of experiments for color. Use the basic unit of 10 grams, adding certain percentages as plus figures. Remember that .1 of a gram is 1 per cent of 10 grams. The colors will be influenced by the quantities of colorants used, by the kiln temperature, by the basic frit ingredients, and by the kiln atmosphere.

Some oxides can be combined with others or calcined alone; these often offer interesting color variations. Examples of such oxides are potassium dichromate, iron chromate, red lead chromate, burnt sienna, and burnt umber. To make most maroon, crimson, and pink glazes, tin oxide, a frit containing calcium, and a commercial maroon, crimson, or pink glaze stain (prepared glazed pigments) should be used. For strong yellows, use commercial stains with a frit containing no calcium; an addition of tin is also desirable in such glazes.

You may find that your glazes are speckled. The speckles are concentrations of color caused by insufficient grinding. Many feel that these are desirable but if you find a lack of uniformity in color objectionable, talk to your supply dealer about acquiring a ball mill.

On pages 98 and 99 are given a number of base glazes which fire at different cones, for which materials are presented in parts by weight, along with a table of ingredients for making colored slips and also for adding color to the base glazes.

STRAIGHT-LINE AND TRIAXIAL BLENDS

There are two very simple methods for developing new glazes from glazes for which you already have the composition. The first of these is the straight-line blend, the second is the triaxial, or trilinear, blend. These blends can be used as a means of either blending colors or of developing variations in texture. They can also be used to develop a glaze that will mature at a temperature different from that of any of the parent glazes. For example, by combining a cone 06 glaze, a cone 02 glaze, and a cone 5 glaze in a triaxial blend, you can doubtless develop one or more glazes that mature at cones 05, 04, 03, 01, 1, 2, 3, and 4. This estimated spread may be a bit optimistic, but not excessively so. In a straight-line blend, a similar

spread in maturing temperatures can be achieved by combining two glazes that mature at different temperatures.

PREPARING STRAIGHT-LINE BLENDS

First select the two glazes you wish to blend, mix an equal quantity of each, and place each glaze in a separate covered jar labeled with its identifying symbol and the composition of the glaze. Since this type of blend involves only two glazes, the identifying symbols commonly used are "A" for the first glaze and "B" for the second.

To determine the results of firing straight-line blends consisting of varying amounts of glazes A and B, you can simply make and fire a series of test tiles coated with blends of various proportions of the glazes. Eleven such tiles can be made using the percentages illustrated in the nearby diagram of a straight-line blend. In the diagram, the box at the extreme left represents test tile #1, which should be coated with 100% of glaze A. Test tile #2 is represented by the second box from the left. This should be coated with a straight-line blend consisting of 90% glaze A and 10% glaze B, and so on through the entire series to test tile #11, which should be coated with 100% glaze B.

Label the back of each test tile with its representative number from 1 to 11 as you apply the glaze. All labeling should be done with a Drakenfeld ceramic marking pencil (see Suppliers List). After the glaze coatings are dry, fire the test tiles to the desired cone.

PREPARING TRIAXIAL BLENDS

The triaxial blend is used to determine the percentage composition when three glazes are combined. The glazes are identified by symbols "A," "B," and "C." The triaxial blend may represent an almost unlimited number of combinations of the glazes, but for our purposes, the 21-point triaxial blend illustrated in the nearby diagram should be adequate. In this diagram, point 1 represents 100% of glaze A, point 16 represents 100% of glaze B, and point 21 represents 100% of glaze C. Each successive space between one of these three points and the next line of numbers represents a 20% decrease in the amount of that particular glaze and a 20% increase in the amount of one or both of the other two glazes. For example, as you move from point 1, which represents 100% of glaze A, to point 2, you lose 20% of glaze A and replace it with 20% of glaze B. Point 3, which is also one space away from point 1, represents a loss of 20% of glaze A and an addition of 20% of glaze C. Points 4, 5, and 6 are each two spaces away from point 1. Therefore, the composition of glaze A is decreased a total of 40% at each of the three points; 40% of glaze B is added at point 4; 20% glaze B and 20% glaze C are added at point 5; and 40% glaze C is added at point 6.

The nearby table describes the percentage compositions of each glaze designated by each of the 21 points. You can test these triaxial blends as you did the straight-line blends. Simply weigh out the correct percentages of glazes A, B, and C for each of the 21 compositions, mix them together with water, apply them to the test tiles, and fire to the desired cone. Be sure to label the back of each tile with the correct composition number.

Rough-textured stoneware with glaze decoration.

TABLE FOR MIXING DECORATIVE SLIPS

To 100 grams of white firing pottery and modeling clay

ADD:	TO MAKE:
4 grams iron chromate	Gray
4 grams Mason Brown Stain #204	Brown
10 grams red iron oxide	Red-brown
4 grams Mason Blue-Green Stain #7	Blue-green
1 to 4 grams chromium oxide	Green
15 grams Mason Pink Underglaze #163	Pink
5 grams Blue Stain	Blue
4 grams cobalt oxide	Dark blue
5 grams Ceramic Color & Chem. Co. Yellow Stain #1335	Yellow
6 to 8 grams Black Stain	Black

To prepare for use: Mix and grind ingredients in mortar and put through 80-mesh screen. Add water to make thick cream consistency; thin for spraying.

CHART OF % OF OXIDE ADDITIONS TO FRITS OR BASE GLAZES SHOWN

Antimony oxide	2%
Cobalt oxide	1%
Copper oxide	2%
Chromium oxide	1%
Crocus martis	4%
Molybdenum oxide	2%
Manganese oxide	2%
Nickel oxide	2%
Red iron oxide	4–8%
Rutile	5–10%
Tin oxide	5–10%
Vanadium oxide	2%

Note: A larger percentage will darken the color; less will make it lighter.

Glaze I. Cone 06-04. Orange (gloss red specks). Trent Thompson

White lead	42.4
Soda ash	7.4
Lithium carbonate	5.1
Potassium carbonate	3.5
Whiting	1.9
Kaolin	13.4
Flints	26.3
	100.0

Chromium oxide	.25
Molybdenum oxide	1.50

Note: Better specks when sprayed.

Glaze II. Cone 06-04. Textured gloss. Bob Noll

Plastic vitrox (PV clay)	50
Colemanite	50
	100.00

Add to 100.00%:

Red iron oxide	4.
Manganese carbonate	1.
Rutile	7.
Vanadium oxide	10.

Glaze III. Cone 05. Imitation stoneware. Bob Noll

Del Monte spar	28.2
Nephelene syenite	21.2
Borax	1.3
Colemanite	6.0
Fluorspar	11.2
Lithium carbonate	5.8
Zinc oxide	2.7
Flint	11.3
Strontium carbonate	11.3
EPK	15.0
	115.0

Add:

Red iron oxide	4.0
Manganese	1.0
	120.00

Note: Rough when thin; velvety when thick.

Glaze IV. Cone 02. Semi-matt. Nancy Lynch

White lead	31.2
Potassium carbonate	7.1
Whiting	5.4
Zinc oxide	6.1
Clay	25.8
Flint	24.3

Note: May develop pitted texture when heavy.

Glaze V. Cone 02. Semi-gloss. Jan Jones

White lead	34.4
Pearl ash	6.3
Whiting	2.1
Barium carbonate	13.1
China clay	22.7
Flint	21.4

Glaze VI. Cone 2. Slightly fluid matt. Jan Jones

Nephelene syenite	46.65
Whiting	18.15
Zinc oxide	14.89
Magnesium carbonate	.16
Clay	1.33
Flint	19.02

Glaze VII. Cone 2. Waxy matt. Nancy Lynch

Nephelene syenite	44.9
Magnesium carbonate	4.0
Zinc oxide	2.9
White lead	25.1
Clay	22.3
Flint	.8

Glaze VIII. Cone 2. Gloss. Robert Smith

Kona A-3 feldspar	66.80
Soda ash	.16
Whiting	4.46
Zinc oxide	2.23
White lead	26.32

Glaze IX. Cone 5-6. Leadless barium matt. Warren Westerberg

Del Monte feldspar	60.9
Whiting	13.2
Barium carbonate	25.9

Note: Good in either oxidation or reduction. Very good for colors.

Glaze X. Cone 5. Fluid leadless opalescent glaze. Mary Auvil

Frit #3110	52.32
Colemanite	13.38
Whiting	.05
Lithium carbonate	1.31
Strontium carbonate	10.50
Kaolin	10.69
Flint	11.75
Rutile	4% addition

Note: Excellent with coloring oxides. Do not apply too heavily. Good in oxidation or reduction fire. Best over dark body; also fires good glossy coat at cone 2.

Glaze XI. Cone 5-6. Waxy semi-gloss. Joan Bugbee

Del Monte spar	89.04
Whiting	2.76
Barium carbonate	5.47
White lead	2.73

Note: For excellent opaque semi-gloss add 8% tin plus coloring oxides. For waxy matt add 10% rutile and coloring oxides.

Glaze XII. Cone 5. Dead stony matt. Fred Lucero

Kona F4 feldspar	113.4
Zinc oxide	19.2
Barium carbonate	35.1
Clay	18.6
Flint	11.8
Rutile	1.9

Glaze XIII. Cone 5. Textured mottled semi-gloss glaze. Trent Thompson

Kona F4 feldspar	37.79
Whiting	9.82
White lead	21.87
Lithium carbonate	1.05
Kaolin	14.20
Flint	15.27
	100.00
Vanadium oxide	2% addition

Note: Grind glaze, add vanadium and stir in, then apply with a brush. Good in oxidation or reduction. Eggshell in oxidation, darker in reduction.

Glaze XIV. Cone 5. Cecile McCann

Nephelene syenite	55.73
Barium carbonate	15.83
White lead	12.94
Lithium carbonate	2.47
Boric acid	1.56
Kaolin	1.73
Flint	9.76

Note: Good in oxidation firing. In reduction, with addition of 1.5% copper oxide, .25% Cr_2O_3, will give reds where thin, greens where thick; CuO plus $CoCO_3$ gives red and blue. If mixed and used immediately, glaze has a very smooth texture. If used after standing for several days, glaze will give a bubbled, blistered surface.

Glaze XV. Cone 7. Gloss glaze.
Robert Smith

Nephelene syenite	63.80
Dolomite	8.47
Whiting	4.61
Zinc oxide	11.20
White lead	11.88

Add 5% tin oxide and coloring oxides.

Glaze XVI. Cone 7. Dry matt.
Joan Bugbee

Nephelene syenite	56.34
Barium carbonate	24.02
Whiting	19.64

Note: Lithium carbonate, soda ash, and potassium carbonate are soluble in water, so glazes containing these materials should be stored dry and when mixed with water used immediately.

Straight Line Blend
A Simple Blend of Two Glazes

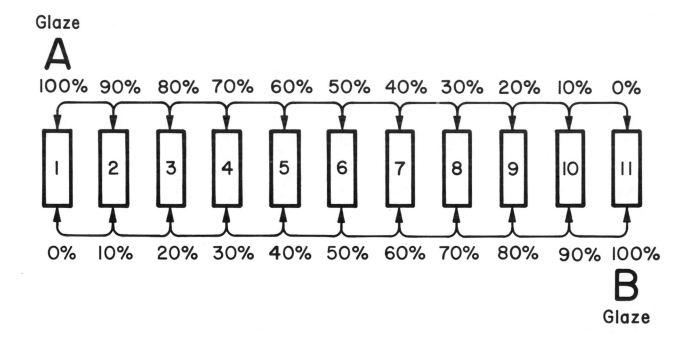

In this diagram of a straight-line blend, the percentage composition of Glaze A increases by 10% with each step to the right; that of Glaze B decreases by 10% with each step to the left.

Triaxial Blend

A Blend of Three Glazes

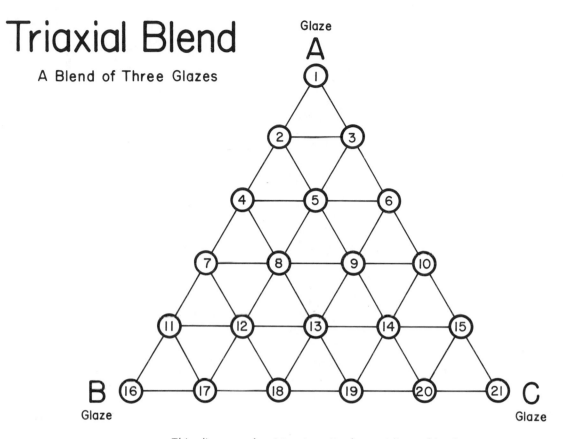

This diagram of a 21-point triaxal, or tri-linear blend represents the blend of three glazes of 20% variations of each glaze.

TRIAXIAL PERCENTAGES

Point	Glaze A	Glaze B	Glaze C	Point	Glaze A	Glaze B	Glaze C
1	100%			12	20%	60%	20%
2	80%	20%		13	20%	40%	40%
3	80%		20%	14	20%	20%	60%
4	60%	40%		15	20%		80%
5	60%	20%	20%	16	0%	100%	
6	60%		40%	17		80%	20%
7	40%	60%		18		60%	40%
8	40%	40%	20%	19		40%	60%
9	40%	20%	40%	20		20%	80%
10	40%		60%	21			100%
11	20%	80%					

(Right) Matching pitchers made on the wheel. Clay is stoneware, glaze seaweed ash.

(Below) Stoneware casserole with glossy brown glaze. Doug Cotterall

9
Wheel-Built Forms

It is not known when or where clay ware was first formed on the potter's wheel. Credit for the invention of the wheel has been given to most of the great cultures of the past—very early Chinese pottery pieces show marks indicating use of the wheel, and paintings on Egyptian tombs and Greek vases show that wheels were used for pottery making—but it may or may not have been an independent discovery in each country.

The potter's wheel has undergone many changes in form. In China and Japan the handwheel, as well as the kickwheel and the electric wheel, are in use. The large circular head of the handwheel has holes around the periphery; the potter seated before the wheel inserts a stick into one of the holes and turns the wheel until it revolves rapidly. An American variation of the handwheel is the Milbrandt wheel model M-2 (see Suppliers List). It is quite inexpensive and permits you to sit while potting.

A type of wheel commonly adapted for studio use today is the kickwheel, with its head fastened to an upright shaft over a heavy flywheel. The shaft is attached at the bottom to a treadle that moves horizontally. The potter stands on his right foot before the wheel and turns the wheel by pressing and releasing the treadle with his left foot. Another foot-operated wheel is commonly known as the European kickwheel. The wheelhead is set at the top of the upright shaft, and a large, heavy flywheel or circular disc is mounted on the bottom of the shaft to turn on a horizontal plane. The potter sits on a bench built as part of the wheel and operates the wheel by kicking the lower disc with the ball of his right foot, which sets both upper and lower discs to turning in a counter-clockwise direction.

The primary advantage of using a kickwheel is that it allows for the control of speed. Today a variety of electric wheels also have variable speed controls. In general, however, electric wheels are much more expensive than kickwheels and handwheels.

If you have a knack for carpentry and a measure of ingenuity, you can readily build a wheel of your own. You can improvise the wheel assembly from used automobile parts, bought at a wrecking yard. The wheel should be mounted absolutely level in a sturdy housing. A successful home-built wheel is shown in Chapter 12.

The steps used in making pottery forms on a wheel are known as throwing and are the same regardless of the type of wheel used. Mastery of the wheel may take considerable practice but it provides the same challenge to the craftsman as those presented by the important phases of any worthwhile craft. Keep in mind that today's master potters were also once beginners.

CLAY FOR THROWING

The clay you use for throwing can be the same as that used for other methods of building. Pottery clays with or without a small addition of fine grog may be used. Thorough wedging of the clay is important in this method; it should be moderately stiff, completely uniform in texture, and free of lumps or air bubbles. Lumps, hard or soft, or incorporated air bubbles will distort the form being thrown. Expect porcelain to be somewhat more difficult to manage on the wheel because of its fine-grain quality.

TOOLS FOR THROWING

The first of these is a suitable wheel. Others are a sharp ice pick or awl for trimming cylinder rims, a length of piano or other strong, fine wire for cutting forms loose from bats or the wheelhead, and a trimming tool for turning excess clay from form bottoms, etc.

Accessory needs are plaster bats or aluminum plates to set over the wheelhead when throwing, a pan or bowl to hold water close to the work for lubricating the hands and clay while throwing, and sponges for lubricating, smoothing, and clean-up operations. One sponge should be a small "elephant ear," the best shape for smoothing finished ware.

THROWING

A thrown piece of pottery is formed by the potter's hands while the clay revolves as an integral part of the wheelhead. The head is usually a metal disk which revolves on a horizontal plane—as truly horizontal as possible, or true verticals cannot be achieved in throwing. The metal disk may be aluminum, brass, iron, or steel, but preferably a non-rusting material. Some potters prefer to do the throwing directly on this metal disk; others cover it with aluminum plates which have holes placed to fit over set-screws in the wheelhead, or simply fasten plaster bats to the wheelhead with clay slip. Added bats or plates have an advantage in that they can be removed without cutting the thrown piece loose at the bottom; this makes it easier to recenter the piece for trimming. The beginner is advised to use removable bats or plates.

BEGINNING THE THROWING PROCESS

Start by wedging a mass of clay about the size of an indoor baseball or a little larger. Pat and smack the clay into a round, smooth ball. Slap the ball lightly onto the center of the wheel, using sufficient force to flatten it slightly on the bottom. The metal heads should be dry when the clay is put on them for throwing, or the clay will slip and slide instead of turning as an integral part of the wheel—which it must do. A plaster bat should be moist when the clay is put on it or the clay may come

BOWL. 1. *Sprinkle ball of clay to lubricate.*

4. *Exert uniform pressure from all sides.*

7. *Keep fingers stiff, bend wrists outward.*

2. Under pressure, clay rises to make cone.

3. Flatten cone with downward pressure.

5. Make well by pressing left thumb in mound.

6. Remove excess water from well with sponge.

8. Flare bowl sides with gradual pressure.

9. Note how wall is spread between hands.

CYLINDRICAL FORM. 1. Start by making well.

2. Left-hand fingers press wall on inside.

3. Right-hand knuckle presses against outside.

4. Bring hands slowly upward to pull up wall.

5. If wall spreads, collar it in both hands.

6. Leave wall slightly thicker at bottom.

loose from the bottom when the piece is only partly formed. Help the clay cling to either the plaster or metal surface by first patting the ball all around, then pressing it down toward the wheelhead until you have a cone-shaped mound. This will also prevent water from getting between the clay and the metal plate.

CENTERING

The first step in throwing is centering the ball of clay on the wheelhead. Start the wheel turning counter-clockwise. When it is turning quite rapidly, dip your hands in water and clasp the clay mound in both hands. Exert uniform pressure from all sides until the clay spins smoothly and shows no irregular motion as the wheel revolves. Lubricate the clay and hands as often as needed; if the clay drags under your hands, centering it will be impossible. Brace your left elbow firmly against your body and hold your left forearm rigid as you press the lower part of your left palm against the clay. The combined weight of your body, arm, and hand will force the revolving clay to the center of the wheel. Use your right hand to sprinkle water on the clay and to pull it toward you as your left hand presses it away from you.

Under this pressure, the clay will rise in a cone. Some potters spin the clay into a cone, then press it down by flattening it with the thumbs several times before forming the low, flattened mound which is the starting shape for forming the cylinder. The cylinder is the basic shape from which all other thrown forms are developed. It will be worthwhile to practice making cylinders before attempting other forms.

MAKING THE WELL

This is the next step after the ball is centered and shaped into a low, flattened mound. Support the mound with your right hand and clamp the fingers of your left hand over the right, with your left thumb tip resting on the center of the clay mound. Insert your left thumb into the mound, leaving enough clay between the thumb and wheelhead to form the bottom of the piece.

SPREADING THE BALL

When the well is made, you are ready to spread the ball. This is done with hands held in the same position as for making the well but with the left thumb brought toward the supporting hand; this

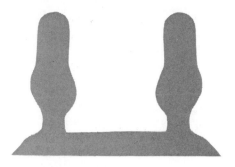

When clay forms slight bulge, draw up.

Think of arms and shoulders as a C-clamp.

causes the clay to flow and expand ahead of the thumb. When the ball is spread to make an opening of the desired diameter for the inside bottom of the piece, you are ready to pull up the walls of the cylinder.

PULLING UP THE CYLINDER

When the clay ball is spread to form the inside bottom of the piece, lubricate your hands and the clay and place your left hand inside the opening with the fingers extended and cupped slightly. Permit the ends of your fingers to rest on the inside bottom, with the pads against the wall. Double your right hand to make a loose fist—notice the cushion thus formed by the side of first finger at the second joint. It is this cushion that does the work on the outside of the cylinder. Rest the knuckles of your fist against the wheelhead at the bottom of the clay and start the wheel. Exert pressure uniformly with both right and left hands. As soon as the clay forms a slight bulge above your fingers, you have pressed hard enough. Without increasing pressure, bring your hands slowly upward, pulling or pushing the clay bulge ahead of them.

To help keep the pressure uniform, think of your arms and shoulders as forming a C-clamp. "Lock" this C-clamp and then draw up your hands to form wall. Do not stop the pulling-up process in the middle of the cylinder wall at any time, or the finished piece will have irregularities in wall thickness. Start at the base, holding your hands in position, and draw them up and above clay; then release. Repeat to make the walls higher and thinner until all the clay from the ball has been drawn into the cylinder.

The cylinder should be straight and vertical. You may find that the form tends to spread at the top. To control this, contract the cylinder top after each pulling-up by encircling the outside of the piece with both hands and pressing the wall inward. The wall of the completed cylinder should be slightly thicker at the base than at the top. If the wall is higher on one side of the piece than the other, or if one side of it is thicker than the other, it means that clay was not perfectly centered at the start of the throwing. Slight unevenness in the rim can be trimmed away with the ice pick or a similar tool. To trim, support the clay edge between the first finger and thumb of the left hand and brace the end of the ice pick against the right thumb, with the point about ¼" from the top of the cylinder wall. As the wheel revolves, press the point of the pick through the clay to cut it off.

SHAPING THE CYLINDER

There are a few standard operations which apply in the development of any form made from a thrown cylinder on the wheel. The wheel speed should be rather slow and hands comparatively dry even when lubricated. Your left hand should be inside the cylinder with the ends of your fingers directly opposite those of the right hand, which should be on the outside of the pot. Pressure from the inside fingers expands the form while those on the outside restrain it. Pressure from the outside will cause the form to contract at the point of pressure. It is usually best to draw the form in by applying uniform opposing pressures with the fingers of both hands.

Do not attempt to develop the form in one operation, but repeat the process several times. After each operation, study the developing form and work in the desired refinements in contour in successive operations.

To finish the form, smooth and burnish the outside by holding the ball of the first finger of the right hand against the revolving shape. Inside support should be furnished throughout the finishing by the ends of the fingers of the left hand.

If the piece sags, lacks symmetry, or looks unpleasantly heavy, the clay may have become too wet during the throwing, or the wall is of uneven thickness or was made too thin.

MAKING A FLARED BOWL

To make a bowl from the cylinder, first decide on the approximate shape. A flared bowl is formed by extending the fingers of both hands and using the entire surface of the hands and fingers to form the bowl. Keep your fingers stiff and close together. Place your left hand inside the cylinder with the fingers resting on the bottom and the palm against the wall. The right hand is placed directly opposite on the outside of the wall. Bend the wrist to spread the cylinder at the top, pressing the clay wall to form from the inside. The outside hand acts as control and guard. Plates are developed in much the same way, from low cylinders.

OVOID AND SPHEROID FORMS

To make an ovoid (egg-shaped) or spheroid (round) form, use your left hand, slightly cupped and with the finger pads against the base of the inner wall, to oppose the right hand on the outside. Apply medium pressure at the base of the wall, in-

FINISHING. 1. To trim bottom, invert on wheel.

2. Center and anchor in place with coil.

3. Use trimming tool to cut away excess clay.

4. Recess bottom of piece to make foot rim.

5. Shave lightly to refine outlines of shape.

6. Sponge to remove cutting tool marks.

PITCHER. 1. First step: pull up cylinder.

2. Round form with pressure from inside.

3. Draw top in with pressure from outside.

4. Trim and round top edge, flare slightly.

5. Sponge and smooth completed form.

6. Form lip between thumb and fingers.

creasing it as you approach the central area to cause the wall to expand. As your hands near the top, gradually decrease the pressure from the inside and increase it from the outside. Repeat this forming process several times until the desired results are achieved.

When any wheel-made form is complete, sponge the edge of the rim with a wet elephant-ear sponge to smooth and round it slightly and set the piece away to dry until leather-hard.

To make duplicate forms—a set of cups or plates, for example—the clay should be weighed into duplicate amounts.

THE PULLED SPOUT

If the form you have made suggests a pitcher, you can pull a spout in the edge rim. Support the rim on the outside with two fingers of the left hand spread apart. With the first finger of the right hand, stroke the clay upward and outward on the inside of the rim between the two spread fingers. A light downward direction at the rim will help to make the spout a dripless one.

TRIMMING AND FINISHING

The process of cutting and shaving the outside surface of the leather-hard thrown form to perfect profile irregularities and finish it is called either turning or trimming. Trimming is a proper part of the throwing process although skillfully thrown pieces need less cutting and shaving to perfect them; it is the aim of all potters to keep this part of the work at a minimum.

As soon as your thrown pot is leather-hard, return it to the wheel and center it. If loose from the bat, fasten it in place with a coil of clay to trim or refine the top area. Use the trimming tool for cutting, then smooth the piece with wet sponge.

In order to trim and turn a foot in the bottom area, cut it loose from the wheelhead if necessary and invert the form. Center it on the wheelhead and fasten it in place with a coil of clay. Cut the foot rim by recessing the bottom of the piece and do any necessary refining of line in the lower part of the shape. The piece should never be trimmed on the inside.

Let the wheel revolve rather slowly as the trimming process proceeds. Hold the trimming tool at an angle which allows it to cut cleanly without scraping. When trimming is complete, sponge to smooth the cut surfaces and sign your piece on the bottom before you set it away to dry.

PULLED HANDLE. 1. Start with tapered clay wad.

2. Wet hand and pull over clay.

3. Stroking and squeezing lengthens clay.

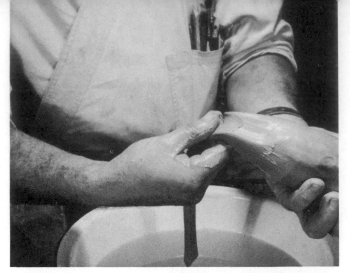

4. *Bend the tapered, pulled strip to make handle.*

5. *Handle may be applied directly to form.*

6. *The pulled handle has a fluid, plastic quality.*

THE PULLED HANDLE

This is the ideal handle for the thrown piece because of its plastic, fluid quality. To make a pulled handle, wedge a quantity of stiff but plastic clay and pat it into a tapered wad. Grasp the heaviest end of the wad tightly in the left hand. Wet your right hand with water and pull it over the tapered clay with a gradually tightening squeeze. This downward stroking, squeezing motion, done repeatedly, will cause the clay to lengthen. The shape of the lengthening strip is controlled by the pulling of the right hand and the position of the fingers throughout the operation. The tapered part of the strip is used to make the handle; the thicker part forms the top of the handle.

The pulled handle may be applied directly to a leather-hard form. If it is too plastic for immediate application, it can be dried somewhat on a plaster bat.

If the handle is applied immediately after pulling, the surface of the leather-hard pot should be prepared by scoring the surfaces where the top and bottom of the handle will join the pot. These surfaces should then be wet and allowed to set for five minutes before the handle is attached. If the handle has been permitted to harden slightly, heavy slip instead of water should be applied to the scored surfaces on the pot.

In planning a handle for any piece, try to make it a size and shape that will suit the piece in both function and appearance. Imagination must take the place of an actual test for function, as the piece obviously cannot be lifted by the handle at this stage. Remember, too, that the space enclosed by the handle is a part of the design and should be carefully planned to fit the shape and size of the piece upon which it is placed.

LIDS AND SPOUTS

Lids and spouts add to both the design and function of the thrown piece. They can be thrown and trimmed on the wheel or formed as slabs. The teapot illustrated nearby shows the steps in making a thrown spout and lid.

WHEEL-MADE SCULPTURE

Nothing will give you more feeling of accomplishment than your first successful thrown sculpture.

In thrown sculpture forms, all unnecessary detail is eliminated and the plastic quality of the forms is emphasized. For your first attempts you should make many sketches or drawings of the sculpture

THROWN SPOUT. 1. Form on wheel to plan.

2. When stiffened, cut at desired angle.

3. Mark position on leather-hard form.

4. Pierce strainer holes within outline.

5. Score and paint joints with slip.

6. Seal joints with pressure from tool.

FLANGED LID. 1. First, measure opening.

2. Check measurements with calipers.

3. Fit flange and place lid on form.

4. Center pot, trim curve of lid top.

5. Prepare lid top and knob for joining.

6. Attaching knob completes teapot.

SLAB SPOUT. 1. Plan with paper pattern.

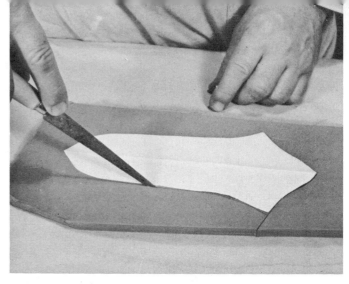

2. Use pattern for cutting clay shape.

3. Position on form and mark.

4. Pierce strainer holes in lower area.

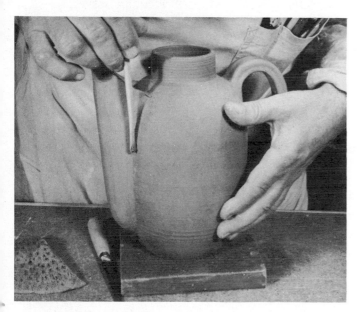

5. Score, add slips to joints, model firmly.

6. Sponge and smooth joint on finished form.

Stoneware wheel sculpture entitled "The Trophy."
John Leary

you wish to make. Sketches help to establish dimensions and proportions of the various forms and their relationship in the completed sculpture. Later you may wish to design each form on the wheel as you go, but this procedure requires some background or experience.

Once you have established dimensions and proportions, you are ready to throw the various forms. The foundation unit should be thrown first. This provides a basis of comparison for related forms or appendages. Next throw the related forms in scale with the foundation form. All forms to complete the sculpture should be thrown during a single working period and placed in a closed box or cupboard. As soon as the clay does not stick to your fingers, all necessary trimming should be done and the pieces assembled. In assembling the forms, try to retain a thrown quality throughout. If possible, avoid cutting the foundation piece or you will decrease its strength. Check all appendages against the foundation form for position and size, and cut them to fit. Apply the appendages by deeply scoring the joining surfaces and coating the scored areas with heavy slip. Press the joining surfaces firmly together with a slight rocking motion, increasing pressure until they are solidly joined. Permit the resulting ridge or bead of slip pressed out of the joint to remain in place until leather-hard, then clean it carefully away. Avoid carving or scraping the thrown form; if flattened areas are desired, press them gently but firmly into shape before joining the pieces. If necessary, appendages can be curved or bent after they are in position. If they have become rigid, wrap them with damp cheesecloth until they are plastic enough to bend. Any closed forms should have concealed vent holes to permit enclosed air to escape during drying.

The pair of chickens shown nearby were made by George Eimers and are each composed of a bottle form closed at the top and two sections of a conical form. The sections of the cone make the base and tail for each bird. The forms were trimmed and assembled as soon as they had reached the early stages of leather-hardness and could be handled without losing shape. In assembling, the bottle form was tipped at the desired angle and mounted on the narrow section of cone. Both the base and area on the bottle to be joined were scored and coated with slip, then pressed and worked solidly together, after which all the edges were welded. The second section of cone was then cut to fit and joined in the same manner. The beak, comb, and wattles were the last parts applied. The beaks are solid cones modeled by hand, and the combs and wattles are made from slabs of clay. The clay used was an especially compounded body that contained 10 percent manganese dioxide. The result is a grayed purpled-brown matte surface, unglazed.

The ping pong trophy made by John Leary is equal in complexity to the chickens. The body, base, and head are each individually thrown pieces. The body is a cylindrical bottle form and the head is a spheroid vase form, while the base is an inverted, flat-bottom bowl.

The pieces were thrown and trimmed; when leather-hard, coils of clay were attached to outline the coat and hair. The arms were attached as coils, after which the hands were modeled. The paddle was made from a slab, the ball from two pinch bowls joined at the rims. The thrown crown was carved when leather-hard, and the ornamentation was then added and modeled. The nose was a coil, and the eyes were balls of clay pressed into depressions in the head.

The parts were assembled by scoring their edges and sticking them together with thick slip. The undergarment and the edges of the coat and hair were impressed with stamps and painted with red iron oxide; the writing was impressed with type. After biscuiting, the coat, paddle, ball, and crown were glazed and the piece was reduction fired to cone 9. Later, the paddle, ball, and crown were painted with liquid gold and the piece was fired to cone 020.

When you make sculptures on the wheel, always try to retain the thrown quality of the forms in the finished product. This does not mean that the forms cannot be flattened or pressed into variations of the original thrown shape if desirable or necessary. It does mean, however, that carving or elaborate modeling of the forms only detracts from their appeal as thrown sculpture. Such pieces would be more pleasing if made by a process more in keeping with the result.

Hen and Rooster, wheel sculptures. J. George Eimers

WHEEL SCULPTURE. 1. Thrown parts needed for Bull.

2. Apply slip to scored areas.

3. Press neck firmly into place, then weld.

4. Place head in position.

5.. Leg ready for assembly. Note vent holes.

6. Sgraffito pattern on coating of black slip.

COIL-AND-THROW PROCESS

The coil-and-throw process is an ancient Korean technique still used by some potters in Japan. To make a large bowl by this process, pat out a pancake of clay on the wheel. Use coils 1" in diameter. Turn the wheel as you build 3" to 5" of the cylinder. Smooth the coils with damp hands as wheel turns. Let the piece set for an hour or two, add four or five more coils, smooth, and let set again. When the cylinder is two-thirds of its final height, expand the form to one-third the finished width. Add the final coils and finish shaping. (Coil-and-throw demonstration by Joe Hysong.)

COIL AND THROW. 1. One-inch coils build cylinder.

2. Smooth coils with damp hands as wheel turns.

3. After hardening, add 4 or 5 more coils.

4. When 2/3 final, expand to 1/3 finished size.

5. When all coils added, throw to final shape.

119

THROWING FROM A MOUND

Throwing from the top of a mound saves time when making small pieces. Warren Westerberg demonstrates the process in the nearby illustrations. Roughly center a large quantity of clay in a cone-shaped mound. At the top, center the amount required for the form. With the thumb and first finger of your left hand, make a groove below the centered top. Support the centered portion with your hands as both thumbs make a well and spread the ball. Pull up the cylinder and shape it. Cut the piece loose with nylon thread.

MOUND THROWING. 1. Center top of mound.

2. Support clay as thumbs make well, spread ball.

3. Pull up the wall.

4. Cut form from mound with nylon thread.

5. Lift from mound with both hands.

THROWING LARGE FORMS

Sometimes the clay required to throw a large piece is more than you or the wheel can handle. To make large forms, throw several sections, one at a time, and assemble them as shown in the series nearby, or coil and throw the form. Either method takes practice.

SECTIONAL FORMS

To make a form from several sections, you need a pair of calipers; the joining sections must all have the same diameter and wall thickness (except for the last, or top, section, whose wall should be thicker than those of the others). The first section is a cylinder with a bottom; the other sections are

SECTIONAL FORM. 1. Score joining surfaces and coat with thick slip.

2. Invert the second section and press it firmly into position.

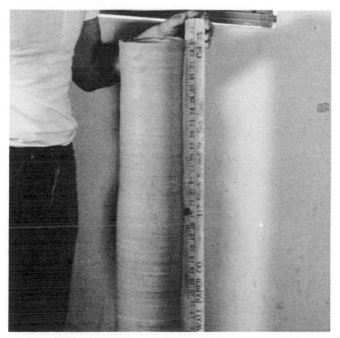

3. Cut plate loose with wire, add third section. Three sections assembled are 34" high.

4. Throw neck from thick wall at the top of the cylinder.

TWO CENTERS. 1. *Throwing on new center distorts symmetry.*

2. *Finished form has neck to one side.*
Non-symmetry of thrown forms may be emphasized by paddling when leather-hard.

Fluting just after throwing by stretching clay from inside with finger develops non-symmetry.

thrown without bottoms. Throw all sections and carefully check the joining diameters with calipers. Set the sections aside as you finish, and let them set until they have hardened enough to support one another. They should be hard enough at an early stage of leather-hardness. Deeply score the joining surfaces and join them together with thick slip. Leave the last section, with the thicker wall, at the wheelhead. Press the sections firmly together and weld the joints inside and outside. The joints can be paddled with a downward dragging motion of the paddle from one section to another while one hand supports the inside wall. Invert the thick-walled section, moisten it, and throw the neck. When leather-hard, trim any irregularities, cut the form from wheel, and attach it to the piece. (Demonstration of sectional forms by Jan Jones.)

ASYMMETRICAL FORMS

You can develop pleasing variations in symmetry by pressing with your hands, by paddling, or by fluting with your fingers immediately after throwing or when the form is leather-hard and trimming is completed.

Asymmetry can be developed in a form thrown on two centers. To make such a form, throw a cylinder the size and wall thickness for the completed pot. Move the metal plate or plaster bat so that the cylinder is off-center. Fasten the plate or bat in the new position with wads of clay and complete the shaping.

Thrown, paddled bottle that shows incised decoration. Claude Horan

Cast birds of red earthenware with gray speckled, semi-matt glaze. Copper wire comb wattles. Elliott House

10
Cast Forms

Clay wares can also be formed by the casting process. In this method, liquid clay that has been specially prepared for this purpose, known as "casting slip," is poured into a highly absorbent plaster mold.

The dry, porous walls of the mold draw the water out of the clay next to it, causing it to solidify. The clay in the center of the mold, however, remains liquid. When the clay next to the mold has thickened sufficiently to form a wall, the liquid is poured off, leaving the clay form perfectly fitted to the mold.

This method enables the potter to make a large number of copies of an original model and is used extensively by pottery manufacturers. It also permits the studio potter to make hollow, thin-walled forms not easily made in other ways.

A simple one-piece mold will provide the best starting place for your experience in making pottery forms by casting. You will need a quantity of potter's plaster and mixing equipment for it (see Chapter 3); a piece of Masonite and linoleum or tar roofing paper strips to make an enclosure for the plaster; liquid soap, Vaseline, or mold soap to coat any parts of the plaster enclosure which might otherwise stick to the plaster; your ordinary clay and tools; casting slip; and an original model.

Since casting slip is more than merely a diluted mixture of clay and water, it is recommended that you get complete instructions from your clay supplier before attempting to make your own slip. Otherwise, you should buy prepared slips from a ceramic supply house. Store slip in a closed, airtight container.

MAKING A ONE-PIECE MOLD

First make the form to be duplicated. It must not have undercuts or reverse curves, and its diameter must be not greater than that of the top of the piece or you will not be able to remove it from the one-piece mold. Shallow bowls or wide-mouthed vases can be successfully cast in this type of mold. Make your original shape by any of the methods described so far in this book, and allow it to become leather-hard. It should be smooth and free of bumps, particularly on the outside, as the outside of your model will be duplicated on the inside of your plaster form—which in turn will be the outside surface of the finished cast piece.

Prepare to cast a mold of your original model by first rolling a clay slab about 2" thick on a Masonite or linoleum foundation. Use dividers to mark out a circle the same size as the top of the leather-hard clay form. Using the original center, mark a second circle ½" larger than the first. Cut along the line of the outer circle with a fettling knife tipped so that the clay edge takes an outward angle and the clay forms a flat, tapered plug. Invert the model on the plug, fitting the rim to the outline of the smaller circle.

Next make an enclosure around the assembled plug and model. Use a strip of linoleum, tar roofing paper, or heavy cardboard to make a cylinder at least 2" larger all around than the plug and at least 2" higher than the model. Tie the cylinder at top and bottom with strong cord—tie it around the middle as well, if the plaster mold is to be large.

1. Put model inside form.

2. Pour in Plaster.

3. Fill mold with slip.

4. Remove clay plug.

Place the cylinder over the plug-and-model assembly so that the margin around it is even, and secure the cylinder in place with a coil of clay pressed around the outside bottom. Seal the outside vertical joint with another clay coil. Remove the model from the plug temporarily to enable you to seal inside the bottom and vertical joint with a clay coil; then replace.

Coat the inside surfaces of the form, including the Masonite edge extending beyond clay plug, with soap or Vaseline.

Estimate the quantities you need and mix the plaster according to the directions given in Chapter 3. Pour it into the cylindrical enclosure and over the model and plug. Fill to the top with as little splashing as possible—let the plaster flow over your fingers at the edge of the cylinder to break its fall—striving to keep air bubbles out.

When the plaster has set undisturbed for an hour, peel away the clay coils and cylinder and remove the plug and the original clay model. Scrape the outside edges of the mold to remove any plaster fins or chips and let it dry in a warm room for at least a week before using.

USING THE MOLD

When your mold is dry, set it on a level surface and pour it full of prepared slip. This should have a consistency like that of heavy cream. Stand by to add more slip as the level of the original pouring sinks. The mold absorbs water from the slip so that a clay wall begins to thicken next to the plaster, and the mold must be kept filled with slip until this clay wall is of the desired thickness. This thickness will depend on the size and character of the piece being cast, but it should be about ¼" on your first pieces. You will be able to see the thickness of the drying layer as it forms next to the plaster.

When the wall has attained the desired thickness, pour out any clay that is still liquid and invert the mold with its clay lining over a heavy wire screen or slats laid over a pan to catch the clay drippings. Allow the clay to drain for about one-half hour. Then set the mold upright and scrape and clean the rim of the casting with a wooden modeling tool. This will help it to dry evenly, without pulling or warping, as the piece hardens. As it hardens, it will pull away from the mold to show a parting crack between the plaster and the clay form. When the clay is stiff enough to handle without fear of misshaping, remove it from the mold.

The impression of the clay plug in the mold will leave a clay margin or collar on your original clay form. When the casting is removed from the mold, trim this collar away and permit the form to dry until leather-hard. Sponge the rim with a damp elephant-ear sponge and set it away to dry before biscuit-firing.

THE SOLID CAST ASYMMETRICAL FORM

To make a solid cast asymmetrical form, first model the form that will constitute the hollow of the bowl on a piece of Masonite. Turn this model upside down on the Masonite, then draw the proposed outline of the outer edge of the form on the Masonite with an indelible pencil. Build a clay wall ½" thick along the outside mark of the penciled line, using large coils of plastic clay; make the wall at least ½" higher than the center form. Mix and pour plaster over the form to fill the space within the clay wall to the top.

As soon as the plaster has set, remove the clay wall and cut and trim the still pliable plaster to the shape desired for the outside of the bowl or container. There should be no undercut sections on this type of casting form. When the plaster is completely hard, smooth it with sandpaper and sponge any loose particles from its surface. Also sponge the Masonite foundation.

Coat the plaster model and surrounding Masonite with three coats of soap or Vaseline, allowing an interval of about fifteen minutes between each coat..Wipe the plaster surface lightly with a sponge or soft cloth to remove any excess Vaseline or soap. Make a tapered clay plug about 2" long and approximately 1" in diameter at the small end, and fasten it at center of the widest part of the bowl bottom.

Next construct an enclosure around the plaster model. This can be a rectangular frame 2" larger on all sides than the model. Make it from boards supported by bricks and tie around the board frame with heavy twine. Seal the bottom edges inside and out with clay coils; seal the inside corners in a similar manner.

Mix and pour plaster into the enclosure, filling it until ¼" of the clay plug extends above the plaster surface. When the plaster has set, remove the frame enclosure and turn the mold over. Remove the clay mound from the center of the plaster model and cut V-shaped keys on the top sides of the mold.

Apply several coats of Vaseline or soap to the mold surface, keys, and the depression left by the removal of the clay mound. Sponge or wipe clean as described earlier.

Reassemble the wooden frame enclosure around the model and pour the second half of the mold to a depth of 2". When the plaster is set, separate the mold halves and remove the clay plug. Let the completed mold dry as previously described.

To use the mold, fasten the halves of the mold firmly together by tying them with heavy cord or securing them with several 1" bands of rubber cut from an old inner tube. This mold will serve you in two ways: it can be used as a drain mold, as well as for making solid castings.

For drain casting, fill the mold with slip by pouring it through the hole formed by the plug. Check the wall thickness as the slip hardens by gently scraping the walls of the plug. Continue adding slip as the original level falls. When the wall reaches the desired thickness, invert and drain the mold. When the clay wall parts from the plaster mold, remove the mold, trim the walls of the clay plug from the piece, and smooth away any marks left by the joint of mold, etc.

To make a solid cast piece with this mold, pour it full of casting slip, continuing to fill it as needed until the drain hole is filled with a solid plug and there is no core of liquid clay. The solid cast form will take longer to harden than the drain-cast form. When the plug has pulled away from the surrounding plaster, take the mold apart and remove the cast form. Sponge with a damp elephant-ear sponge and permit it to dry completely before firing.

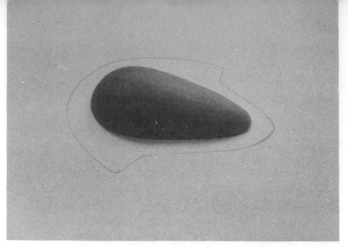

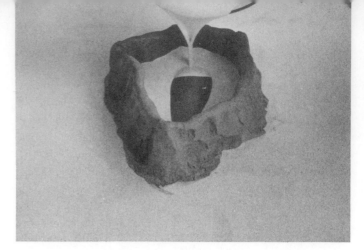

TWO-PIECE MOLD. 1. *Make clay mound to form bowl inside; draw outside edge.*

2. *Form clay dam around outside line; pour plaster over clay mound.*

5. *Pour plaster into cylinder, level with end of clay plug. This forms half of mold.*

6. *Remove mold from form, turn it over, and cut keys into it to lock with other half.*

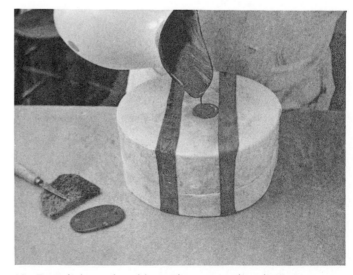

9. *Remove model from plaster molds. Note keys for aligning halves of mold.*

10. *Tape halves of mold together, pour clay slip into drain hole.*

3. Carve and model the plaster casting until it takes desired shape.

4. Add clay plug to plaster model, dress with soap, and place in cylindrical dam.

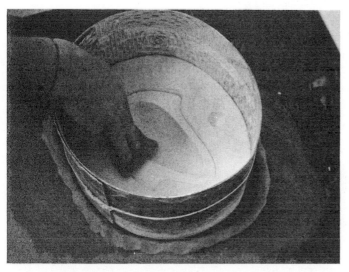

7. Remove clay mound from mold, replace mold inside dam, and dress with soap.

8. Pour 2 inches of plaster on top of first mold to form second half of two-part mold.

11. Pour excess slip out of mold, let clay dry; then separate halves, trim casting.

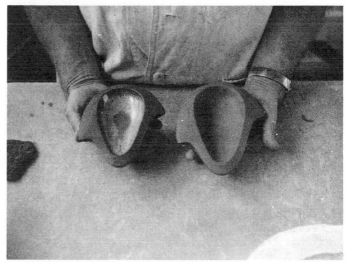

12. Smooth and trim cast clay form, then fire. Note shrinkage of form after firing.

Kiln holds load of glazed pieces. Note cones.

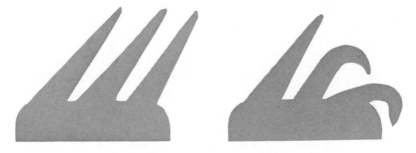

Unfired and fired pyrometric cones.

11
Firing
the Kiln

Few craft experiences offer more satisfaction than taking perfectly fired ware from the kiln. It is a satisfaction not dulled by the occasional piece which is, for one reason or another, somewhat less than perfect. The firing process tests your skill in building ware, and it is firing that makes a dried clay shape become a durable form.

If you are a beginner working at home or in a class, your first pieces will probably be fired in a kiln operated by someone else. However, you will probably be interested in knowing something about kilns and how they are fired, as you may own and operate a kiln eventually.

KINDS OF KILNS

There are several kinds of kilns, which may be referred to according to such features as the fuel used; the operating phases, such as "periodic" or "continuous"; or as being of the "open" or "muffle" variety.

In the home, schools, or studios, the kiln will be a periodic one—stacked with ware, fired to the maturing point for the ware, cooled, drawn, then stacked and fired again. The continuous kiln, kept in constant operation over long periods of time, is used industrially. The open kiln is also largely industrial.

In this type of kiln, flames and smoke circulate through the firing chamber and the ware being fired is sometimes placed in fireclay boxes known as saggars, which protect it from the smoke and flames.

There are two types of open kilns: updraft and downdraft. In recent years a variety of open kilns designed for schools and craftsmen have become available. These kilns are chiefly of the updraft type and may be used for either oxidation or reduction firing. They come in a variety of sizes, so there should be one available to suit your needs. Through a change of orifice on the burner, these kilns can be adapted to use either natural or bottled gas.

In the muffle kiln, the ware is protected from smoke, flames, and fumes by the muffle that surrounds the firing chamber. In this kiln the ware is stacked on shelves made of fireclay and is heated by radiation from the muffle wall. Present-day muffle kilns use oil or gas as fuel and are most commonly used in schools and studios.

The electric kiln provides the cleanest possible firing conditions; muffles and saggars are not needed since flames and smoke are absent. Heat is provided by radiation from several types of electric elements: Nichrome wire and Nichrome ribbon, both of which are nickel chromium alloys; in the Globar kiln, a carborundum rod; and the Swedish Kanthol element, the composition of which is unknown.

The small electric kiln with a Nichrome element is recommended for home use. It will take less room than most household appliances, can be plugged into the ordinary wall socket, and because it is small, firings can be frequent and firing periods relatively short. Temperatures obtained in kilns that operate on ordinary house wiring circuits are necessarily lower than those reached under other conditions, but they will prove adequate for many clays and glazes customarily used in the practice of ceramics as a hobby.

KILN FURNITURE

The interior of the unloaded kiln is a bare, open area and you will need a few pieces of kiln furniture before the space can be efficiently filled with ware. This furniture consists of slabs made of fireclay; posts of varying heights and sizes to support the slabs and thus form interior shelves in the kiln; and various stilts, pins, and buttons to hold glazed pieces up and away from direct contact with shelves or kiln bottom. How many shelves, posts, or stilts you need will depend on the kiln size and the type of load. When purchasing even a small electric test kiln, it is advisable to acquire at least one shelf and four supporting posts, plus a few stilts and pins. All of these are available from your ceramic supply dealer (see Suppliers List).

STACKING THE KILN

Really efficient loading or stacking of the kiln may take practice. For economy of operation and most even heat distribution in the firing chamber, put as many pieces in it as you can. Keep these things in mind, however: leave at least ½" open space between the shelf edges and the muffle wall or electric elements; leave at least ½" space between the walls and the ware, and from ¼" to ½" space between all pieces of glazed ware. Pieces of greenware, without glaze, can touch one another. Small bowls or cups can be placed directly in larger bowls, and cups can hold a handful of beads or buttons for the first, or biscuit, fire. (For this reason, you will find that biscuit-firing a single piece will cost less than having the same piece glost-fired.) It will be wise to avoid placing a very heavy piece on top of one with thin walls.

As mentioned earlier, glazed pieces must not be allowed to touch in the firing. As it becomes molten, the glaze may swell and bubble out from the glazed surface. Moreover, glazes will fuse to make "Siamese twins" of separate but touching pieces, usually to the ruination of both. Another point to note in handling and stacking glazed ware is the necessity of supporting the pieces on the stilts, pins, and buttons to keep them away from shelf surfaces or the bottom of the firing chamber. Glaze fuses to shelves, too, if it runs from the sides of the piece and drips onto them. In glost-firing, shelves should be further protected from stray glaze drippings by a coating of "kiln wash" painted on with a brush. You can buy this wash as a powder and mix it with water to a thin paste. Apply a generous coat or two for safety. Lifting glaze drippings will pull the wash loose, but chipped wash is easily patched.

PYROMETRIC CONES

In all firing, biscuit or glost, the potter makes use of pyrometric cones. These are slender, trihedral (defined by three planes meeting at a point) pyramids made of a mixture of ceramic materials graded to correspond to a progressive series of fusion points. They are numbered from 022, the lowest of the series, through 021, 020, and so on, up (temperature indications go up, although the figures become lower) until 01 is reached. There is no cone 0, but the series then continues as cone 1, 2, 3, etc., up to 42. This is the last of the series and represents a temperature far exceeding the needs of the average potter.

In the nearby table, the fusion temperatures are shown opposite the appropriate number of the pyrometric cone. It should be understood, however, that cones do not measure temperature. Instead, they measure the amount of heat-work done within the kiln up to the time of their melting and consequent deformation. When the tip of the cone collapses (with the heat, so to speak), it means that clays and glazes have reached the required time-temperature conditions and have matured.

Pyrometric cones are necessary because of this time-temperature relationship. If you have ever boiled an egg, you will know that you can bring it to the same degree of hardness by simmering it several minutes in water over a low fire, or by rapidly bringing the water to a galloping boil over a high flame. The size of the pan, the number of eggs, the amount of water—all these are factors that count in arriving at a breakfast egg of just that degree of hardness you desire. So it is in the kiln. A slow, gradual heating of the ware will bring it to maturity at a lower temperature than would be necessary if the heating were rapid. A large and completely loaded kiln will take longer to reach a certain temperature than a small one holding only a few pieces. A peek into the kiln to see how the cones are reacting to the internal conditions will reveal important clues to the progress of the firing.

Pyrometric cones are usually set in the kiln in series of three. They must be made to stand up by being inserted in a small rectangular wad of clay. There must be a "spy hole" in the kiln to allow observation of the cones during firing, and they must be placed on a shelf or post so that they can be seen from the spy hole. Large kilns have more than one spy hole, usually one at the front and one at the back; small kilns have a hole in the front only. A series of cones may be placed at several vantage points in a large kiln, as parts of the kiln may become hotter than others and consequent allowances must be made.

As an example of how cones are used, let's say that you will fire to cone 06. Many clays and glazes are adequately matured at this cone, and it falls within the temperature range possible for a small electric kiln. You should buy standard-size cones in numbers 05, 06 and 07. The 07 cone will respond to the effects of time and temperature first. It is the "warning" cone, and the melting and curling over of its tip indicates that the kiln's contents are approaching maturity. This cone should be set into the right end of the clay rectangle at the angle shown in the diagram on page 135. The curling of cone 06 announces that the fire should be turned off; this should be set at the center of the clay. The left-hand cone, number 05, is the "guard" cone and will not become deformed if the heat is withdrawn at the proper time.

Make up several cone plaques at a time if you consistently fire to the same cone—a good idea for the beginner—and allow the clay bases to dry completely and thoroughly before using. The clay should include some grog to reduce its shrinkage. If the cones shrink more than the clay during drying and firing, they may loosen and fall out. If they shrink less than the clay, they may break off at the base. If all this sounds complicated (although it is really quite simple), buy some cone holders from the ceramics supply house.

FIRING

When the kiln is stacked and the cones are placed so that they can be viewed from the spy-hole during firing, you can begin heating the kiln. Do not close the kiln completely at first. Although the ware may have seemed perfectly dry when you put it in the kiln, green clay and fresh glazes hold "chemical water"; this moisture must be driven off as steam, and the steam must escape from the firing chamber. Leave the peephole uncovered or leave the door ajar until the interior of the kiln is rosy red.

Kilns with fuel controls should have the controls turned up from time to time during the firing. The small electric kiln usually has no controls other than "on" and "off" and simply gets hotter as time goes on. To start such a kiln it is necessary

A. D. Alpine 20-cubic-foot kiln stacked for bisquit fire. This kiln can be used for either oxidation or reduction fire.

CONE AND COMPARATIVE TEMPERATURE CHART

Cone Number	When fired slowly 68°F. per hour Fahrenheit	When fired rapidly 302°F. per hour Fahrenheit
022	1085	1121
021	1103	1139
020	1157	1202
019	1166	1220
018	1238	1328
017	1328	1418
016	1355	1463
015	1418	1481
014	1463	1526
013	1517	1580
012	1544	1607
011	1607	1661
010	1634	1643
09	1706	1706
08	1733	1742
07	1787	1814
06	1841	1859
05	1886	1904
04	1922	1940
03	1976	2039
02	2003	2057
01	2030	2093
1	2057	2120
2	2075	2129
3	2093	2138
4	2129	2174
5	2156	2201
6	2174	2246
7	2210	2282
8	2237	2300
9	2282	2345

only to plug it in. When the first cone deforms stand by to turn kiln off when the middle cone is down. Do not, under any circumstances, open the door of any kiln until it is completely cool. The resulting cold shock to the hot ware may cause it to crack or shatter—a danger not only to the contents of the kiln but also to you.

Most gas-fired muffle-type kilns have pilot lights in addition to the burners. The proper procedure in starting such a kiln is to turn on the pilots one at a time, lighting each from underneath the kiln or with a torch inserted in the firebox. When the pilots are lit, the burners are turned on low, one at a time until all are operating; then the pilots are turned off. If necessary, turn up the burners every two or three hours until the appropriate cone has deformed. Adjust the burners to a clean blue flame throughout the firing. A yellow flame indicates that the mixture lacks air, and this may cause blistering of glazes or a condition within the kiln known as "reduction," which affects glaze colors. Excessive gas may also cause glaze defects such as sulfuring or scumming.

Each kiln has a temperament and personality of its own. You can learn how to get the best results from a particular kiln only by experimenting with it. Size and type, as well as kind and size of load and fuels, determine how long it will take to bring any kiln load to maturity. A small electric test kiln holding few pieces may need only two or three hours to reach the desired heat. If the electric kiln is larger and equipped with a switch that allows the heat to be turned on low, medium, and high, it should probably be heated at low for one or two hours, at medium for a similar length of time, turned on high until the firing is completed, then turned off immediately.

Take particular care in firing with gas and such combustible fuels. Should gas burners go out at any time during the firing, turn off all gas and wait a day before relighting pilots or burners.

Before purchasing any kiln, gas or electric, be sure that it is constructed to fire safely at temperatures you want to reach. In other words, if you want to use cones that call for temperatures above 2000 F., check the specifications for the kiln to see if the linings and elements are designed to withstand this heat without damage. Kilns last longer if consistently fired at less than the stated maximum temperatures. Electric elements burn out in time but are replaceable.

OXIDATION AND REDUCTION FIRING

The above discussion of firing emphasizes oxidation, a type of firing in which there is more oxygen in the ware chamber than is needed for the body and glaze to remain in their normal condition as oxides of the various elements. The atmosphere for oxidation firing is composed primarily of carbon dioxide plus oxygen.

The next type of firing is the Oriental middle fire, or what we call neutral fire, in which there is just enough oxygen in the ware chamber to form carbon dioxide.

The third type is reduction firing, in which the atmosphere is composed of carbon dioxide plus carbon. The free carbon is greedy for oxygen and robs the coloring oxides of a part or all of their oxygen, causing a color change.

Low-temperature glaze materials, particularly the lead compounds, are less stable than the materials used in glazes that fire from cone 5 to cone 10; therefore reduction at lower temperatures is seldom desirable and may result in blistered glazes. Reduction at high temperatures may cause a subtle change in the textural quality of such a glaze, as well as increased richness and a change in color. True reduction firing requires an open-type kiln, either updraft or downdraft. Do not attempt reduction in your electric or muffle kiln unless you are quite experienced and are sure there are no fire hazards.

Home-made potter's wheel has optional elbow rest.

12
Building a Potter's Wheel

Many potters prefer an electrically driven wheel. However, most wheels of this type have the disadvantage of running at a constant speed—a handicap to the beginner who needs control of speed at all times. Variable-speed motors are available, but they are expensive. The home-assembled wheel illustrated here gives speed control with a ¼-horsepower motor (quite inexpensive). The motor operates the wheel by friction drive.

The motor and a foot pedal are mounted on a hinged shelf underneath the bench. A rubber-tired wheel on the motor shaft presses against a large disc, which serves as a flywheel to turn the potter's wheel. The assembly requires a metal shaft and bearings, two plywood discs, and a sturdy wooden frame to house the operating unit.

You can pick up the metal parts at a machine shop or a junkyard. You will need some help from a machinist to fit the shaft into the bearings unless you can find parts that already fit, or unless you have a lathe and metal working equipment of your own. Make the shaft from any straight piece of metal that can be machined. (It should be at least 1″ in diameter.) Use an automobile axle if you find bearings to fit it. If you have the shaft turned by a machinist, use a piece of steel that is slightly softer than that in an auto axle.

You can buy bearings wherever used auto and appliance parts are sold. Use a crankshaft bearing where the shaft connects with wheelhead. Any type of thrust bearing may be used at the bottom where the shaft attaches to the flywheel.

Both the 12″ wheel and the 28″ disc for the flywheel in the assembly illustrated nearby were made of ¾″ plywood. (Use marine plywood, and paint each side with linseed oil to waterproof it and prevent warping.)

To make the flywheel sufficiently heavy, weight it with an old flat-belt pulley 18″ in diameter. Drill holes through the spokes of the pulley wheel so that it can be bolted to the underside of the disc. Since the wheel is powered by friction drive, no belts are required. The flywheel can also be used as a kickwheel. Some potters may prefer a heavier wheel; if you do, attach a larger flat-belt pulley to the plywood disc and fill in the spaces between the spokes with cement.

The hinged shelf on which the motor is mounted is held up away from the flywheel disc by a short expansion spring. The foot pedal is mounted at the right front edge of the shelf. Pressure on the pedal against the spring permits the shelf to drop. The rubber-tired wheel on the motor shaft presses against the plywood disc and turns it. The amount of pressure applied to the pedal determines the wheel speed.

The small drive wheel should have a set-screw so that you can fit it onto the motor shaft yourself; or have a machinist mount the small wheel for you. On this motor-drive wheel, use a rubber tire designed for model autos, available at hobby shops. Add a friction brake as shown, if you wish, holding it up with a screen door spring. You can stop the wheel as you like with foot pressure.

Two-by-fours were used for the wooden frame. These were joined with lap and half-lap joints and fastened with two machine bolts and two metal washers at each joint. The frame dimensions can vary. Make the height and the distance between

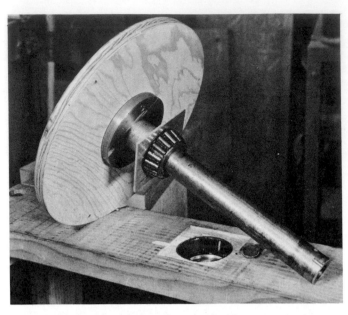

the table and bench to suit yourself. The bench seat is built on an incline to help you lean toward your work.

You can buy plaster bats or cast your own to use on top of the wheelhead. Use the aluminum discs which come in some craft woodworking equipment. These are held on the wheelhead by three pegs.

If you would rather not bother hunting for parts for your wheel and don't mind the extra expense, you may be able to buy a shaft, two sets of steel ball bearings, an aluminum head, and a cast iron flywheel to assemble into a home-built frame. It is also possible to buy a throwing head set with a ¾" bore. Check hobby shops or surplus stores in your area, or try such sources that sell by mail order. Mail order scientific instrument suppliers are another possible source.

Underside of potter's wheel. Note automotive-type bearing used here.

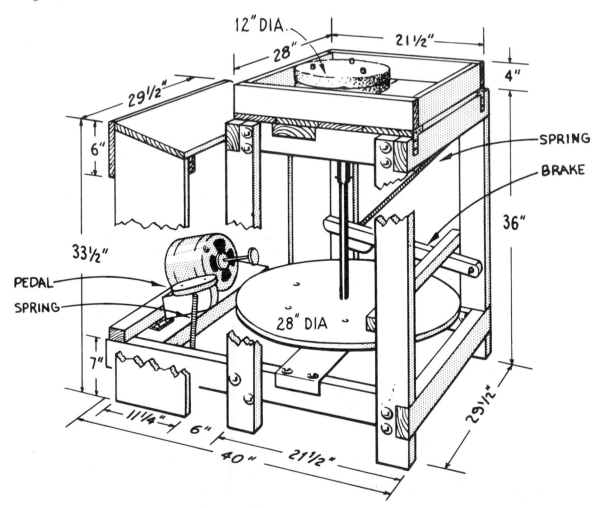

Note two springs. One holds motor drive up off flywheel, other holds up brake shoe.

Bibliography

Berensohn, Paulus. *Finding One's Way with Clay.* New York: Simon and Schuster, 1973.

Binns, Charles Fergus. *The Manual of Practical Potting,* 5th Ed. London: Scott Greenwood and Son, 1922.

Butler, A. J. *Islamic Pottery.* London: Ernest Benn Ltd., 1926.

Cardew, Michael. *Pioneer Pottery.* London: Longman Group Ltd., 1969.

Dodd, A. E. *Dictionary of Ceramics.* New York: Philosophical Library, 1964.

Fraser, Harry. *Electric Kilns.* New York: Watson-Guptill, 1974.

————. *Glazes for the Craft Potter.* New York: Watson-Guptill, 1974.

Green, David. *Pottery Glazes.* New York: Watson-Guptill, 1973.

Harvey, Roger, and Kolb, Sylvia and John. *Building Pottery Equipment.* New York: Watson-Guptill, 1974.

Leach, Bernard. *A Potter's Book,* 7th American Ed. Hollywood-by-the-Sea, Florida: Transatlantic Arts, Inc., 1956.

Nelson, Glenn C. *Ceramics: A Potter's Handbook.* New York: Holt, Rinehart and Winston, 1971.

Rhodes, Daniel. *Clay and Glazes for the Potter,* Rev. Ed. Philadelphia: Chilton, 1973.

Sanders, H. H. *The World of Japanese Ceramics.* Tokyo: Kodansha International, 1966.

Trevor, Henry. *Pottery Step-by-Step.* New York: Watson-Guptill, 1966.

List of Suppliers

A. D. Alpine
353 Coral Circle
El Segundo, California 90245

American Art Clay Co.
4717 West 16th St.
Indianapolis, Indianapolis 46222

George Fetzer Ceramic Supplies
1205 Seventeenth Ave.
Columbus, Ohio 43211

High Studios, Ceramic Consultant
24700 Highland Way
Los Gatos, California 95030

Lanny Milbrandt
1929 Viola Road N.E.
Rochester, Minnesota 55901
(the Milbrandt wheel)

Newton Potter's Supply, Inc.
96 Rumford Avenue
West Newton, Massachusetts 02165

Rowantree Pottery
Blue Hill, Maine 04614

Sculpture House
38 East 30th Street
New York, New York 10016

Standard Ceramic Supply Co.
Box 4435
Pittsburgh, Pennsylvania 15205

Western Ceramic Supply Co.
1601 Howard St.
San Francisco, California 94103

Westwood Ceramic Supply Co.
14400 Lomitas Ave.
City of Industry, California 91744

Jack D. Wolfe Company, Inc.
724 Meeker Avenue
Brooklyn, New York 11222

Index

Edited by Lois Miller
Set in 10 point Optima
Printed and bound by Halliday Lithograph Corp.